Straight from the Fridge, Dad

A Dictionary of Hipster Slang

Max Décharné

NO EXIT PRESS

Acknowledgements

To Ion Mills for saying yes to the book proposal in the first place, to Derek Duerden, Margaret Duerden, Geoffrey Openshaw, Ann Scanlon and Cathi Unsworth for help and inspiration, and to Ant Hanlon and Stewart Pannaman for all the solid sounds down through the years.

Thanks also to John Whitfield, Claire Munro and Sophie Braham for letting me clutter up their office at a time of no sleep and not enough beer.

A very special thank you to Mark Rubenstein of New York (a prime source of the hep, the gone and the downright wig-tightening), and to Nicole Hofmann, Joe NcNally, Zoe and Mr. Wax who passed the good word along.

Most of all, thanks to Katja Klier, for photography, living space, food and encouragement, without whom this book just couldn't have been written.

Für Katja

direkt aus dem Kühlschrank

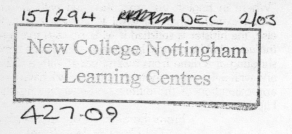
First Published 2000 by No Exit Press Ltd.
18 Coleswood Road, Harpenden, Herts, AL5 1EQ
www.noexit.co.uk

A CIP catalogue record for this book is available
from the British Library.

ISBN 1 84243 000 9

Typeset by Palimpsest Book Production Ltd,
Polmont, Stirlingshire
Printed by Omnia Books Ltd, Glasgow

Introduction

"Where in English we are concerned with communicating *exactly* what we want to convey and nothing else, the hipster is satisfied if what he says manages to *include* what he means. Imagine the difference between shooting at a dime from twenty paces with a .22 rifle, and with a 40-gauge shotgun, and you will have a rough approximation of the difference between English and Hip."

From the album *How to Speak Hip*,
Del Close & John Brent c. 1961

Back in the old days before the dawn of colour TV, genuine hepcats like Cab Calloway and Lavada Durst published dictionaries of hipster slang that took a narrower definition than the present volume and, not surprisingly, wound up with booklets that ran for about twelve pages, although the prize award in this department must go to Babs Gonzales, whose *Boptionary* contains a whole fifty-three phrases spread out over two small, but immaculately cool pages. What you have here is something more inclusive, drawing on phrases and words from pulp novels, classic noir and exploitation films, blues, country and rock'n'roll lyrics and other related sources. Millions of people down through the years have happily read the novels of Raymond Chandler without necessarily knowing exactly what a roscoe might be, and generations of Louis Armstrong fans have enjoyed listening to *Struttin' With Some Barbecue,* only occasionally wondering why the great man felt the need to walk around apparently clutching an item of alfresco cooking equipment. If you attempt to use more than a few of these phrases in normal conversation, you'll most likely be shunned by ordinary, decent people or taken away for special tests at a secure establishment in the country somewhere. Nevertheless, even though many of the words in this dictionary may be the product of sick-minded individuals inventing hip phrases to fill out the dialogue in numerous low-budget teen films and crime stories, they have a life of their own, and most of them refuse to lie down and play dead.

Half the people trying to write the "Great American Novel" fifty years ago seemed to think that the best way to do that was to employ an over-educated style which would have made Marcel Proust look like someone with a limited vocabulary, whereas no-nonsense pulp products like *Hot Dames On Cold Slabs* by Michael Storme or *Two Timing Tart* by John Davidson had an entirely different audience in mind. Although the works of great writers like Chandler and Hammett are rich in authentic slang, it's also true that some of the tackiest or most obscure pulp hacks provide the best and most individual examples of hip as it should be spoken. The blues and rockabilly performers of the 1950s were often making records for small labels with only a very limited, local audience, so they could get away with using phrases which might mean something to a farming community in Texas but be completely incomprehensible in New York, such as Hank Stanford's version of *She's A Hum Dum Dinger (From Dingersville)* which contains the immortal line "She's long, she's tall, she's a handsome queen / She's got ways like a mowing machine".

Many of the books and much of the music quoted here which are now hailed as classics were sneered at and marginalised as throwaway entertainment for the lower orders, and were often being produced by people who didn't know if their career was going to last out the week. The general law that seems to have applied in such cases appears to be that if you worked for peanuts, starved most of the time and died in almost total obscurity, you are then free to be hailed as a genius. When Jim Thompson died in 1977 none of his books were in print in the USA. Nelson Algren was in a pretty much similar position a few years later at the time of his own death, and, by pulp standards, they were two of the howling great success stories. Hell, even Hollywood came calling on relatively regular intervals. Both writers have now been the subject of extensive reissue programmes, but, on balance, they probably don't care much one way or the other these days.

In general, the language contained here originated either with jazz musicians or gangsters in the early part of the 20th century. There's an enormous amount of crossover between these basic reference points, which isn't surprising, since musicians frequently played in venues run by mobsters, and the tough guys with the machine guns were often fans of the music. The well known tale of Frank Sinatra arriving in Cuba to visit Lucky Luciano and the heads of all the US mafia families in 1947, allegedly carrying a suitcase containing a million green pictures of George Washington, is just one example. Both of these two sections of the community enjoyed going to the movies, so once Hollywood started putting out crime films featuring people like Cagney and Bogart, the language was passed around even more, with many real-life hoods trying to dress and behave like George Raft.

It probably won't escape the notice of the more attentive reader that many of these slang phrases concern drink, drugs, sex and violent crime. Jazz music emerged from the Storyville district of New Orleans, a red light area so wide open that the government sent in the troops in 1917 to close the whole place down, and a life spent hanging round in whorehouses and bargain-basement gambling joints is hardly likely to produce a group of people given to speaking like characters from a Jane Austen novel. Attitudes to women, in particular, sometimes make the average cave man look like a bleeding-heart liberal, but, on the other hand, some of the female characters who show up in film noir and hardboiled crime fiction are sharp as a razor and nobody's fool. Veronica Lake, Gene Tierney, Lauren Bacall and any number of Jim Thompson characters could talk back with the best of them and eat most men for breakfast. Sure, attitudes have changed a lot since those days, but that's true across all sections of society and popular culture – the casual racism of children's comics back in the 1940s is breathtaking to modern sensibilities. The overall tone of hipster slang is a kind of deadpan cynicism – not entirely unexpected from a section of society that often spent much of its time trying to avoid the law and scrape the rent money together. The dark tone and worldview of film noir is all the more understandable when one considers that a great many of the people responsible for the genre had escaped from Europe one step ahead of Uncle Adolf and his playmates. Flouting some aspects of the law didn't seem particularly strange back in the Twenties, once the stern moralists with the big sticks had succeeded in having booze outlawed – a particularly smart move which drove nearly the whole adult population into some sort of contact with organised crime in their search for dishonest refreshment.

The earliest examples of slang given here are from around the turn of the last century, and the most recent are taken from the middle years of the 1960s, which was roughly the time when the people who thought they were cool stopped wearing suits, gave up holding onto each other when dancing, and both sexes started a competition to see who could have the longest hair. All cut-off points are pretty arbitrary, but as a handy frame of reference, you could say that Sinatra's Rat Pack in Las Vegas in the early Sixties represent the end of the hipster era as defined by this book. By 1968, four lovable moptops from Liverpool had decided that what rock-'n'roll really, really needed was a serious injection of brass band music and string quartets, and a hippie fan of theirs named Charles Manson out in California was turning on his Family to the White Album: "Are you hep to what the Beatles are saying? Helter Skelter is coming down. The Beatles are telling it like it is." Cab Calloway would have understood the use of the word "hep" in that last sentence, but he sure wouldn't have been likely to have gone up to any stray flower children on the street in Haight-Ashbury and asked them for the address of their tailor.

For the most part, though, it really doesn't matter very much whether you think *Ocean's Eleven* is the name of a football team, or that The Grifters were the vocal group who recorded *Save The Last Dance For Me*. While it's probably true that the language used in films such as *High School Confidential* bears only a slight relation to the way that drug-crazed gang members actually spoke, it still has something of the authentic flavour of those times. Mostly though, it's just there to be enjoyed, and it's worth it just to imagine hordes of impressionable teenage filmgoers back in 1958 attempting to impress their dates with lines like "Give me an intro to this snake and I'll hitch up the reindeers for you".

Anyhow, I'd better hop in my kemp and take off for the casbah.

Plant ya now, dig ya later,

Max Décharné
Berlin, May 2000

STRAIGHT FROM THE FRIDGE, DAD
A DICTIONARY OF HIPSTER SLANG

A

A-1
The best, top of the heap
"'That's my baby,' I said. 'We'll have our good times. Just you and me and thirty grand; maybe five or ten more if it's an A-1 job.'"
From the novel *Savage Night*, Jim Thompson, 1953

A-Bomb juice
Moonshine liquor

A-ok
Fine, all in order, just right

A double this time, waiter. Your singles keep leaking
The correct way to order drinks
From *Ocean's Eleven*, the novel of the film screenplay, George Clayton Johnson and Jack Golden Russell, 1960

A shape in a drape
Someone who looks good in clothes, is sharply dressed

Abyssinia
See you later (I'll be seein' ya)

Ace
1. Something superlative, the top

2. One dollar

3. A marijuana cigarette

4. A policeman
"'Who's chasin' you, Frankie?'
'The aces. They're goin' to pin the sluggin' on me.'"
From the novel *The Man With The Golden Arm*, Nelson Algren, 1949

5. "An outstanding, regular fellow."
From the booklet *The Jives Of Doctor Hepcat*, Lavada Durst, 1953

Ace in the hole	Something in reserve, an advantage, secret weapon deriving from card players having an ace up their sleeve See the jazz recording *Ace in the Hole*, The Black Diamond Seranaders, 1926
Ace out	Cheat, defraud
Aces up	Something mighty fine, excellent
Action	What's happening eg: "Where's the action, pops?"
Adobe dollar	Mexican peso
Age of pain	Prohibition, the time of the 18th Amendment, which lasted from January 1920 until December 1933
Agitate the gravel	Leave, depart, vamoose
Ain't no sin to take off your skin, and dance around in your bones	Enjoy yourself, get with it, relax
Ain't nothin' you can tell me I don't already know	I'm right, you're wrong, shut up
Alabama lie detector	Police baton
All broke out with the blues	Depressed, low down
All creeped up	Scared, apprehensive, frightened
All-electric	Far better looking than the average "Ordinarily, too, I am not a guy who goes ga-ga on lamping a babe, even though, like this one, she makes it appear that other gals run on gas and she's an all-electric."

	From the novel *Slab Happy*, Richard S. Prather, 1958
All gone	Drunk, intoxicated
All over them like a cheap suit	Sticking really close to someone eg: "That guy at the dance was all over my sister like a cheap suit."
All sharped up	Well dressed, suavely turned out
All shook up	Disturbed, hopped up, excited, real gone "Cool down Eve, you look all shook up." From the novel *Scandal High*, Herbert O. Pruett, 1960
All steamed up like a pants presser	Sexually excited
All wet	Disappointing, worthless
Alligator	1. *Down Beat's Yearbook of Swing*, 1939, lists this as "A swing fan who plays no instrument, or musician who frequents places where orchestras are playing". 2. Hipster term of address, often shortened to Gator. Similar in meaning to Cat or Hepcat
Already slated for crashville	Out of control eg: "We could see that the car was already slated for crashville."
Alreet	In order, fine, very good
Alroot	See alreet
Alvin	A rube, a sucker, an easy mark
Amscray	Run away, leave (backslang for scram)
Ankle	To walk

Ants in my pants	Sexually excited "I'm gonna hug you baby good and tight, now love me baby like you done last night, cause I got ants in my pants, baby for you ..." From the blues recording *Ants In My Pants,* Bo Carter, 1931
Anywhere	Possessing drugs eg: "Is you anywhere?" ie: Do you have any? From the autobiography *Really The Blues,* Mezz Mezzrow and Bernard Wolfe, 1946
Applesauce	Flattery, insincere praise, a load of old flannel eg:"Don't hand me that applesauce, Pops."
Ark	"Dance hall, coliseum, any building for dances, meetings, etc." From the booklet *The Jives Of Doctor Hepcat,* Lavada Durst, 1953
Artillery	Guns
As bare as hell's back yard	Completely empty
As busy as a one-legged tapdancer	Extremely busy
As dead as five cent beer	Dead and buried
As drunk as two sailors	Soused, plastered, three sheets to the wind

As full as a pair of goats

Totally drunk
"Before long we were as full as a pair of goats."
From the short story *The Golden Horseshoe*, Dashiell Hammett, 1920s

Ashes

Having sex
eg: "Getting your ashes hauled."
"She said I could haul her ashes
better than any other man,
she said I could sow my seed
anytime in her ash can."
From *Ash Can Blues*, Bob Clifford
c.1930

"I worked all winter
and I worked all fall,
I've gotta wait until spring
to get my ashes hauled."
From the blues recording *Tired As I Can Be*, Bessie Jackson (Lucille Bogan), 1934

See also *Alleyman (Haul My Ashes)*, Sadie Green, 1926 and *Looking For My Ash Hauler*, Washboard Sam, 1937

Awash

Drunk

Axe

Musical instrument

B

B girl

Bar girl, usually working in a clip joint, whose job is to encourage the customers to buy more alcohol
"Settling down in Baltimore, she found lucrative and undemanding work as a B-Girl. Or, more accurately, it was undemanding as far as she was concerned. Lilly Dillon wasn't putting out for anyone; not, at least, for a few bucks or drinks."
From the novel *The Grifters*, Jim Thompson, 1963

Baby blues

Eyes

Back door man

Lover, someone who sneaks in through the back door when the husband is away
See *I'm A Front Door Woman With A Back Door Man*, a blues recording by Lillian Glinn, 1929

Bad

1. Good

2. Evil

Bag

Your interests, your preferences or habitual doings

Bag man

Go-between, drug dealer, person to whom protection money is paid

Ball the jack

1. To move fast
"Suppose you were riding that manifest out of Denton, the fast meat train that balls the jack all the way into El Reno."
From the novel *Savage Night*, Jim Thompson, 1953

2. Having sex
"'I was pretty obnoxious myself,' Deedee giggled. 'I mean, I don't really think you and Moms were balling the jack together. You know that, Brad.'"
From the novel *Run Tough, Run Hard*, Carson Bingham, 1961

3. Have a wild time, get real gone
See *Ballin' The Jack*, a recording by
The Victor Military Band, 1914
(The following year they recorded a title
called *Blame It On The Blues*.)
See also *Ballin' The Jack*, recorded by
The Louisiana Rhythm Kings, 1929

Bam	Girlfriend, steady date, parking pet
Bandrats	Groupies
Bar-polisher	Habitual drinker, frequenter of gin-joints
Barbecue	Girlfriend, good looking woman

"She faced him now, her eyes blazing,
her face flushed. 'I don't think I
particularly enjoyed your role the night of
the party, either, if you want the honest
truth about it, Brad Dixon! Strutting off
with that blond barbeque the minute you
set foot in the house!"
From the novel *Run Tough, Run Hard*,
Carson Bingham, 1961

Louis Armstrong's Hot Five released a
jazz record called *Struttin' With Some
Barbecue* in 1927.
ie: Dancing with a pretty girl.

Barbecue stool	The electric chair
Barfly	Regular drinker, ginmill cowboy, serious lush-head

See *Bill the Bar Fly*, a country record by
Tex Ritter, 1935

Barrel fever	Drunkenness, a raging thirst
Barrelhouse	1. Gin-joint, taproom, speakeasy, brothel

See jazz recordings *Barrel House Man*,
Elzadie Robinson, 1926 and *Barrel
House Man*, Will Ezell, 1927

2. Style of boogie piano playing

Down Beat's Yearbook of Swing, 1939 calls it "Swing music played in a 'dirty and lowdown' style".

Batter the drag   Beg on the street

Battle axe   Musician's slang for a trumpet

Beanery   No-nonsense food joint

Beastly   Very good

Beat

1. Exhausted, worn out
"Art sounded more than tired, he sounded beat."
From the novel *The Golden Key*, William O'Farrell, 1962

2. Broke, out of cash, tapsville

3. Hipster of the late 1940s and 1950s defined by the literary group around Kerouac, Ginsberg, Corso, etc
"The night was getting more and more frantic. I wished Dean and Carlo were there – then realized they'd be out of place and unhappy.
They were like the man with the dungeon stone and the gloom, rising from the underground, the sordid hipsters of America, a new beat generation that I was slowly joining."
From the novel *On The Road*, Jack Kerouac, 1957

4. To steal

Beat it out   Play it hot, emphasize the rhythm

Beat me Daddy,   Play some boogie-woogie for me
eight-to-the-bar   The left hand basslines in typical boogie-woogie piano feature a driving, eight-to-the-bar rhythm.
"In a little honky-tonky village in Texas

There's a guy who plays the best piano by far,
He can play piano any way you like it,
But the kind he likes the best is eight-to-the-bar,
When he jams it's a ball,
He's the Daddy of 'em all."
From the boogie-woogie recording *Beat Me Daddy, Eight To The Bar*, The Will Bradley Trio, 1942

Beat someone for their bread

Swindle or rob someone
"I knew the cab driver had beat me for my bread, but there was no use crying, it was gone."
From the autobiography *I, Paid My Dues, Good Times . . . No Bread, A Story of Jazz*, Babs Gonzales, 1967

Beat the boards

Tapdance

Beat the gong

Smoke opium

Beat the rap

Escape criminal charges, be found not-guilty
Frederick L. Nebel wrote a story called *Beat The Rap* for the May 1931 issue of *Black Mask* magazine.

Beat the tubs

Play the drums
"It's all in the wrist n' I got the touch – dice, stud or with a cue. I even beat the tubs a little 'cause that's in the wrist too. Here – pick a card."
Frankie Machine lists his accomplishments.
From the novel *The Man With The Golden Arm*, Nelson Algren, 1949

Beat your chops

Talk
"Say, is it a solid fact that you guys can beat your chops, lace the boots and knock the licks out groovy as a movie whilst jiving in a comin'-on fashion?"
Bing Crosby to Nat Cole, US radio, 1945

Beat your gums   Talk
                      "You know, medicine's found ways to
                      prolong some old squares' lives. You
                      know how they spend it? Beating their
                      gums . . ."
                      From the film *Shake, Rattle And Rock*,
                      1957

Beatnik   A word coined by Herb Caen of the *San
                      Fransisco Chronicle* in 1958, for an arti-
                      cle about the Beats. Sputnik, the Russian
                      satellite, was much in the news at the
                      time. Picked up by the media it came to
                      symbolize to the public the jazz-loving,
                      Kerouac-reading, non-conformists of the
                      1950s, but was a term hated by many of
                      the Beats themselves
                      "She had her old beatnik costume on –
                      the tight black pants, the bulky black
                      sweater – and her hair was brushed and
                      her lipstick was bright and straight."
                      From the novel *The Wrecking Crew*,
                      Donald Hamilton, 1960

                      See the vocal group recording *Beatnik
                      Girl*, The Bi-Tones, 1960

Bebop   Modern jazz style devoloped by Charlie
                      Parker, Dizzy Gillespie and others in the
                      early 1940s
                      Dizzy put out a single called *Bebop* in
                      1945.
                      See also *He Beeped When He Shoulda
                      Bopped*, Dizzy Gillespie & his Orchestra,
                      1946; *Poppa Stoppa's (Bebop Blues)*, Mr.
                      Google Eyes & his Four Bars, 1949; *Be-
                      Bop Wino*, a vocal group recording by
                      The Lamplighters, 1953

Bedroom furniture Dame, doll, gasser
                      eg: "She's a swell piece of bedroom
                      furniture."

Beef   1. Complaint, grievance
                      "I'm not beefing about the Saratoga

let-down. The guys we were fishing for just didn't bite."
From the novel *Killers Don't Care*, Rod Callahan, 1950

2. To talk

3. A criminal charge, or a crime

Behind	Under the influence of something
Behind the cork	Drunk, intoxicated
Behind the eight-ball	In trouble, in a difficult spot "'I thought Augie was a particular friend of yours.' 'I thought so, too. And here he puts me behind the eight-ball with you ...'" From the novel *Little Men, Big World*, W.R. Burnett, 1951
Behind the parade	Old hat, out-dated, passé
Behind the stick	Working behind a bar – the stick being the wooden bar-top itself
Belly fiddle	Guitar
Belly gun	Weapon with a short barrel, usually a 32.20, used for shooting someone at very close range
Bellyache	Complain eg: "What are you bellyaching about?"
Belt of booze	A drink
Belting the grape	Drinking wine
Bend someone's ear	Talk, chatter "Anway, thanks for the cheer, I hope you didn't mind my bending your ear." From the ballad *One for My Baby (And One More For The Road)*, Frank Sinatra, live at The Sands, Las Vegas, 1966

Bent out of shape	1. Upset, disturbed
	2. High on drugs or drink
Berries	Something mighty fine "She had black hair an' black eyes an' a figure that looked like a serpent with nerve troubles. Except for the fact that she hadn't had her face lifted she mighta been you favourite film star. That baby was the berries." From the novel *Your Deal, My Lovely*, Peter Cheyney, 1941
Better tune me in and get my signal right	Understand what I'm telling you "Better tune me in and get my signal right Or there'll be no rockin' tomorrow night." From the rockabilly recording *I Got A Rocket In My Pocket*, Jimmy Logsdon (aka Jimmy Lloyd), 1958
Bible-puncher	Clergyman
Big barracuda	An important guy "'Got his name?' 'Morrison – big barracuda.' 'He was D.O.A. Knife cut his heart in half.' 'Nobody did it, nobody saw it.'" From the film *Where The Sidewalk Ends*, 1950
Big chill	Death
Big house	Prison In 19th century England, it was a slang name for the workhouse.
Big house up the river	Sing Sing prison
Big sleep	Death Used by Raymond Chandler as the title of

one of his most famous books, published in 1939, and filmed in 1946 with Humphrey Bogart as Philip Marlowe.

Biscuit snatchers	Fingers, hands
Biters	Teeth
Blab	Talk, give the game away
Blab sheet	Newspaper
Black	Nighttime "Say, you look ready as Mister Freddy this black." Freddy Slack talks hep to Ella Mae Morse during the intro to their 1946 boogie recording *House Of Blue Lights*.
Black & white	Police car
Blackstick	Clarinet
Blast	Telephone call "If you ever come to Riverport, how about giving me a blast on the phone?" From the film *Jailhouse Rock*, 1957
Blast the joint	Smoke dope
Blast yourself wacky	Go mad
Blasted	Drunk, intoxicated
Blasting party	Dope party
Bleating your trap	Complaining
Blind staggers	Drunkenness
Blocked	Drunk or high on drugs
Blonde	"It was a blonde. A blonde to make a bishop kick a hole in a stained glass window."

From the novel *Farewell, My Lovely*, Raymond Chandler, 1940

Blot out   Kill, assassinate

Blow   General term for playing a musical instrument, regardless of type

Blow a fuse   Go crazy, go wild

Blow in on the scene   Arrive, make an entrance

Blow the box   Play the piano

Blow the joint   Leave the building
"Let's blow this joint, the music's dead ..."
From the rockabilly recording *Cast Iron Arm*, Johnny Peanuts Wilson, 1956

Blow the scene   Leave, disappear
"Look, baby, just don't you blow the scene on me! Stick in town or I'll chase you down to hell itself!"
From the novel *Two Timing Tart*, John Davidson, 1961

Blow the works   Spill the beans, tell all

Blow up a storm   Cut loose during a musical number, get hot, play at your best
"Say Fats, a bunch of the kids would like to listen to you blowin' up a storm. Would you let them listen in?"
From the film *Shake, Rattle And Rock*, 1957

See also the jazz novel *Blow Up A Storm*, Garson Kanin, 1959

Blow your jets   Get annoyed, lose your cool

Blowtop

1. A crazy or violent person, someone with a short temper

2. "Fellows who are excellent in their fields especially music and dancing."
From the booklet *The Jives Of Doctor Hepcat* Lavada Durst, 1953

"Ain't that going to be kicks ... listen will you to this old tenorman blow his top."
From the novel *On The Road*, Jack Kerouac, 1957

Boat

Automobile
"Capone motioned at a glossy black convertible job parked curbside. 'That your boat?'"
From the novel *Al Capone*, John Roeburt, 1959

Bobby-soxer

Teenage girl, much given to screaming at Frank Sinatra
The name derives from the fashion for wearing short white socks.

Body scissors

Having sex
"I knew by now that she was the kind of dame you couldn't turn your back on for five minutes without her having a body scissors on somebody."
From the novel *Kiss Tomorrow Goodbye*, Horace McCoy, 1949

Boil my cabbage

Blues slang for sex, much used by the female blues singers of the 1920s
"He boiled my first cabbage and he made it awful hot,
he boiled my first cabbage
and he made it awful hot,
when he put in the bacon
it overflowed the pot."
From *Empty Bed Blues Part 2*, Bessie Smith, 1928
See also the blues recordings *Anybody Here Want To Try My*

15

Cabbage?, Maggie Jones, 1924;
Good Cabbage, Victoria Spivey, 1937

Boiler
Automobile
"We're still talking when this boiler
screeches up and stops on a dime. Out
pops Cooch and walks towards us."
From the short story *The Rites Of
Death*, Hal Ellson, 1956

Boloney
Lies
"A bundle of first-class boloney straight
off the ice."
From the novel *Can Ladies Kill?*,
Peter Cheyney, 1938

Bomb
1. Automobile
"Give a listen. Power man! What a
bomb!"
From the novel *Go, Man, Go!*,
Edward De Roo, 1959

"That red Thunderbird
is the craziest bomb in town ..."
From *Red Thunderbird*, a rock'n'roll
recording by Lynn Howard & The
Accents, 1958

2. A failure, such as a musical or theatri-
cal performance

Bone orchard
Cemetery
See *Bone Orchard Blues*,
a blues recording by Ida Cox, 1928

Boneyard
1. Cemetery
See *Boneyard Shuffle,* a country recording
by The Arkansas Travellers, 1927

2. Auto repair shop, garage
"It's in the boneyard, Molly ...you know,
the boneyard where the elephants go
when they're tired of living."
ie: I've smashed up the car.

From the novel *Run Tough, Run Hard*,
Carson Bingham, 1961

Booster   Shoplifter

Boots laced up tight Hep, righteous, in the know, a suave
customer

Booze fight   A drinking spree
There was a biker gang called the *Booze
Fighters* in Los Angeles just after World
War Two.

Bop   1. To fight
The gang fights in the 1960 film *The
Young Savages* are called *bops* rather
than *rumbles*.

2. To dance
"When I die don't bury me at all,
Just nail my bones up on the wall,
Beneath these bones let these words
be seen:
'The running gears of a boppin'
machine.'"
From *Rockin' Bones*, a rockabilly record-
ing by Ronnie Dawson, 1958

3. Jazz movement originating in the
1940s
The word *Bebop* was shortened to *Bop*
with Charlie Parker's 1947 recording
Bongo Bop.
"At this time, 1947, bop was going like
mad all over America. The fellows at the
Loop blew, but with a tired air, because
bop was somewhere between its Charlie
Parker *Ornithology* period and another
period that began with Miles Davis."
From *On The Road*, Jack Kerouac, 1957

See *Coppin' The Bop*, Jay Jay Johnson's
BeBoppers, 1946 and *Bop's Your Uncle*,
George Shearing, 1947
Jazzman Babs Gonzales had a band in

1946 called Babs' Three Bips and a Bop. Artie Shaw opened a club in New York in 1949 called Bop City.

"See you tomorrow, cats. Same time, same channel, same bop beat . . ."
From the film *Shake, Rattle And Rock*, 1957

Bop kick "To play the new sound in music, the latest dance step."
From the booklet *The Jives Of Doctor Hepcat*, Lavada Durst, 1953

Born tired Lazy

Born under a bad sign Fated, unlucky

Boss Something really good, the best

Bottle babies Drunks
From the autobigraphy *Really The Blues*, Mezz Mezzrow and Bernard Wolfe, 1946
In the short story collection *The Neon Wilderness* (1947) Nelson Algren has the variant bottle boy: "And the simple every-day bottle boy, who fights when he drinks, and he drinks all the time."

Bottle heister A drunkard

Bottle tipper Heavy drinker
See *The Fiddlin' Bootleggers*, a country recording by The Monroe County Bottle Tippers, 1928

Bottle up and go Hit the trail, cut out, vamoose, take a powder
See *Bottle Up And Go*, a vocal group recording by The Enchanters, 1957

Bottom dealer Swindler, someone who deals cards from the bottom of the deck

Bought and sold and done for   Broke, down on your luck

Box   1. Vagina
See the shy, romantic 1950s vocal group performance *Baby Let Me Bang Your Box* by The Bangers, or *Hot Box Is On My Mind*, a piano blues by Kingfish Bill Tomlin, 1929

2. A safe
"Can you bust a box if you have to?"
ie: Can you crack a safe?
From the novel *Carny Kill*,
Robert Edmond Alter, 1966

3. Record player or phonograph

Bozo   1. Idiot, square
Originating from Bozo The Clown, a type of circus performer whose main distinguishing characteristic is stupidity.

2. Ordinary guy, all purpose term of address
e.g. "She is wearin' a lime-green frock that was cut by a bozo that could wield a mean pair of shears."

Bracelets   Handcuffs
"One of the uniformed cops frisks me and snaps a pair of bracelets on my wrists."
From the novel *Killers Don't Care*,
Rod Callahan, 1950

Brain it around   Think it over

Brass rail   Bar or saloon

Brawl   Wild party

Bread   1. Money
"In the bread department I am nowhere ..."

19

From the film *High School Confidential*, 1958

2. Penis
See *She's Your Cook,
But She Burns My Bread Sometimes*,
a blues recording by Bo Carter, 1930

Bread pan
Vagina
"She makes my bread rise
late hours in the night,
I put my bread right in her pan
and I shoves it clean out of sight."
From *Bread Pan (Just My Size)* a piano
blues by Roosevelt Sykes, 1937

Bread stasher
Working stiff, wage slave, someone who
saves for a rainy day

Breadsville
A bank

Break it down
1. Musical term, defined by *Down Beat's
Yearbook of Swing,* 1939 as "To get
hot, swing it, go to town".

2. Spill the beans, speak your piece
"'I'm listening,' he said. 'Break it down.'"
From the novel *Death Is Confidential*,
Lawrence Lariar, 1959

Break it off
Stop talking

**Break out like
the measles**
Go wild, play hot music, swing it

Breakfast uptown
A night in jail

**Breathing natural
gas**
Hep, alert, knowing the score

Breeze
Leave, possibly in a hurry
eg: "Think I'd better breeze ..."

Brew
An alcoholic drink

Bright	Daytime
Bright disease	To know too much
Bringdown	Something or someone depressing
Broadway battleship	New York streetcar
Brush	To ignore someone
Bucket	Prison "I'll stay under cover. He's too stir-wise for me. I smell of the bucket." ie: He is sure to be able to tell that I've just come out of prison. From the short story *Goldfish*, Raymond Chandler, 1936
Bucket of blood	Cheap bar, spit & sawdust joint See *Bucket of Blood*, a piano blues by Will Ezell, 1929
Bucket of suds	Takeaway beer, carried home in a bucket
Bug	To annoy or irritate "I'm sorry, baby, but don't bug me." From the film *The Killers*, 1956 See *Like, You Bug Me,* a vocal group recording by The Quarter Notes, 1958
Bug juice	Moonshine liquor
Buggy	1. Automobile 2. Crazy, short for bughouse (see next entry) "Take your buggy boy friend and clear out of here before I forget I'm a lady." From the novel *Pop. 1280*, Jim Thompson, 1964
Bughouse	Crazy, insane, lost it completely The mob nickname Bugsy derives from this – a crazy guy, a stone killer.

Washington Square in Chicago has long been known as Bughouse Square, as has Union Square in New York.

Build me a drink	Mix me a cocktail
Built	Someone with a good figure " 'You've got six weeks to make her a star.' 'Easy, Fats, it takes time. Rome wasn't built in a day.' 'She ain't Rome ...' " ie: She's built already. From the film *The Girl Can't Help It*, 1956
Bull	Cop, policeman
Bull fiddle	Double bass
Bulletproof	Completely drunk
Bulling	Something good, mighty fine
Bum steer	A bad deal, something wrong, an unlucky break
Bump	To kill
Bump your gums	Talk a lot
Bunco artist	Con man, swindler
Bundle	Bankroll, a quantity of money
Bunk habit	"The practice of lounging around while others smoke opium, and inhaling the fumes." From the autobiography *Really The Blues*, Mezz Mezzrow and Bernard Wolfe, 1946
Burg	Town, city
Buried	1. As drunk as a skunk, plastered

	2. A life sentence in jail
Burn	1. Die in the electric chair

Burn

2. Kill someone
"Max grinned genially. From his jacket pocket he produced a small-calibre pistol, then dropped it back again. 'We want you to burn him, Rick.'
Rick stared at him with slowly growing comprehension. 'You mean kill him?' he finally asked in a husky voice.
'You got the scoop,' Max said."
From the short story *A Hood Is Born*, Richard Deming, 1959

Burn leather

1. Dance
See *The Joint is Jumping*, a jazz recording by Fats Waller, 1937

2. Walk fast or run

Burn me up

Go on, give it all you've got
"Burn me up this time, let's see if we can get a little fire into it."
Elvis to his musicians.
From the film *Jailhouse Rock*, 1957

Burn my clothes

An expression of surprise
"Burn my clothes if it isn't Romeo, our financial backer."
From the film *Dames*, 1934

Burn rubber

1. Drive fast, make a quick getaway

2. Have sex

Burned

1. Annoyed

2. Robbed

3. Killed

Burning with a low blue flame

Drunk, swimming, sluiced to the gills

Busier than a hustler with two bunks	*Extremely* busy
Bust your conk	Work hard, be thorough
Bust your vest	Be big, magnanimous
Bus	Car
Busted	1. Arrested
	2. Broke, poverty-stricken "I'm busted, flat." From the novel *Red Harvest*, Dashiell Hammett, 1929
Busted flush	A bankrupt
Busting into a can	Cracking a safe
Butcher shop	Hospital
Butt me	Give me a cigarette
Butter-and-egg man	Out-of-town big spender, the backer of a theatre show, free with his money and often a sucker See *Big Butter and Egg Man from the West*, a jazz recording by Louis Armstrong's Hot Five, 1927
Button	The lookout in a criminal operation
Button-buster	A braggart or loudmouth
Button your gabber	Shut up
Button your lip	Keep quiet
Buy the farm	To die, peg out, cash in your chips
Buzz	To rob, to pick someone's pocket "Tell you what I'll do, Tiger. I'll give you the names of eight cannons that fit the job and I'll bet you thirty eight dollars and

fifty cents that one of them buzzed this
moll's wallet."
From the film *Pickup On South Street*,
1953

Buzz me   Give me a call on the telephone
"Buzz me, buzz me, buzz me baby,
I'm waitin' for your call ..."
From *Buzz Me*, an R&B jump-jive record-
ing by Louis Jordan & The Tympany
Five, 1946
See also *Buzz Me Babe*, a blues record-
ing by Slim Harpo, 1960

Buzzer   Badge or ID, usually that of the police

By the handles   "Keep it up pal, and six of your best
friends are gonna be carrying you by the
handles ..."
Dean Martin to heckler, onstage at The
Sands, Las Vegas, February 1964

C

C-jag
Cocaine binge
Cornell Woolrich wrote a story called *C-Jag* for the October 1940 issue of *Black Mask* magazine, in which the murderer can't remember what he's done with the body due to an over-indulgence of snow.

C note
One hundred dollars
"In a moment, Colosimo returned. He thrust money at Capone with a flourish. 'Five Cs, for a stake.'"
From the novel *Al Capone*, John Roeburt, 1959

Cabbage
1. Money
"I'm looking for some guys with lots of cabbage and a certain amount of respectability . . . worth shaking down."
From the novel *Murder On Monday*, Robert Patrick Wilmot, 1952

2. 1920s blues slang for genitals

Cackle factory
Lunatic asylum
"'He'd be just the man who might try to con Torelli.'
'Con Torelli! You must have been sprung from the cackle factory. Not even Gunner would try that.'"
From the novel *Darling, It's Death*, Richard S. Prather, 1953

Café sunburn
Pallor
From the autobiography *Really The Blues*, Mezz Mezzrow and Bernard Wolfe, 1946

Cake cutter
Short-change artist, swindler

Calaboose
Prison
"The judge he pondered,
Then turned me loose, sayin'

'Too many winos in my calaboose.' "
From the hillbilly boogie recording *The Wino Boogie*, Bill Nettles, 1954

Call some hogs   Snore

Camisole   Prison slang for a strait-jacket

Can

1. Prison
"I'm fresh out of prison
Six years in the can . . ."
From the country recording *Drink Up And Go Home*, Carl Perkins, 1955

2. Automobile
"'Tony,' said Rico, 'ditch that can and come back for your split.' "
ie: Dispose of the getaway car and then we'll divide up the money.
From the novel *Little Caesar*, W.R. Burnett, 1929

3. Backside, rear end
"Ira Borch – the grinning stranger, a slimy sonofabitch who'd been on my can for six months."
From the novel *Always Leave 'Em Dying*, Richard S. Prather, 1961

Can it

Shut up
"'Mike, you surprise me. I thought you were keen on equal rights and all that jazz.' 'Can it,' he growled. 'You know where I stand at this late date.' "
From the novel *The Bedroom Bolero*, Michael Avallone, 1963

Canary

1. Female singer
"You once had a great nose for finding new talent. Dug up some big canaries, but the booze got in your way."
From the film *The Girl Can't Help It*, 1956

There were also many recordings of real

canaries in the 1930s, often trained to
whistle popular tunes of the day.
"There must be a steady sale for 'actual
canary bird recordings' somewhere,
for there is seldom a month without
at least one release by feathered warblers
. . ."
From the magazine *Phonograph Monthly
Review*, New York, November 1930

2. Police informer

**Cancel someone's
Christmas**
Kill them

Canned heat
Cheap hooch made from a mixture of
alcohol and methylated spirits, much
favoured by hoboes and winos
See the blues recording *Canned Heat
Blues*, Sloppy Henry, 1928

Cannon
1. Gun, firearm

2. Gunman
". . . Dave Moroni, Moron for short, who
had been a minor cog in Murder, Inc.
when Bugsy Siegel had been one of their
top torpedoes. The other guy was a top-
notch cannon who could kiss the dog and
lift your wrist watch between ticks."
From the novel *Darling, It's Death*,
Richard S. Prather, 1953

In the film *Pickup On South Street*
(1953), the word is frequently used to
describe a pickpocket or petty criminal.

**Can't see a hole
in a ladder**
Completely drunk

Cap
To shoot someone

Caper
Robbery, criminal enterprise

Capper
A shill, one who assists a card-sharp in
swindling the suckers

Carve your knob   "To make you know, understand."
From the booklet *The Jives Of Doctor
Hepcat*, Lavada Durst, 1953

Cash in your checks   Die
"For the files, Blackie Gitz is just a
mobster who cashed in his checks, via
three slugs in his back, said slugs being
non-self-inflicted."
From the novel *The Corrupt Ones*,
J.C. Barton, circa 1950

Cat   Dude, hipster, a righteous groover
In 1953 Doctor Hepcat defined a cat as
"A young man who is part of the modern
social whirl, dresses in latest smart styles,
understands all types of music dances and
is accepted."

"There's a cat in town that you might
know,
he goes by the name of Domino.
A long key chain and a diamond ring,
a blue sports car, he's a crazy king,
they love him so, that cat called
Domino . . ."
From the rockabilly recording *Domino*,
Roy Orbison, 1956

See the jazz recording *That Cat Is High*,
Tommy Powell & his Hi-De-Ho Boys,
1936
See also the R&B jump-jive recording *At
The Swing Cats Ball*, Louis Jordan & The
Tympany Five, 1939
Not surprisingly, *Down Beat's 1939
Yearbook of Swing* defines Cats as
"Musicians in a swing orchestra, or people
who like swing music."
See also the jazz recording *Stop The War
(The Cats Are Killin' Themselves)*,
Wingy Manone & his Orchestra, 1941

Cat clothes   Hipster threads – serious clothing, not for
the squares

See the rockabilly recording *Put Your Cat Clothes On*, Carl Perkins, 1956

Cat house	Brothel
Cat's pyjamas	The best, top of the heap
Catch a handful of boxcars	Hop a freight train and leave town
Catting around	Playing the field, philandering
Caught in a snowstorm	Addicted to cocaine
Century	One hundred dollars
Chalk-eater	A gambler who always backs the favourite in a horse race
Charging a bank	Robbing a bank "Kid, we got us a little bank in Cedars just itchin' to be charged. It's all cased properly." From the film *They Live By Night*, 1948
Chassis	Body, limbs, etc
Chat'n'chew	Restaurant, hash house
Cheaters	Eyeglasses, spectacles
Check the beat	Listen to the music
Check the character	Look at that person over there From the film *High School Confidential*, 1958
Chew the scenery	Overact, make a big deal of something
Chicago lightning	Gunfire
Chicago overcoat	Coffin
Chicago piano	Machine gun

Chick

Girl, dame
"Dean had arrived the night before, the first time in New York, with his beautiful little sharp chick Marylou."
From the novel *On The Road*, Jack Kerouac, 1957

"Let me tell you bout my real gone chick,
She's got a different style ..."
From the rockabilly recording *Tongue Tied Jill*, Charlie Feathers, 1956

See the vocal group recording *That Chick's Too Young To Fry*, The Deep River Boys, 1945 (Also covered by The Prisonaires, from the Tennessee State Penitentiary, some of whom had wound up behind bars for exactly the reasons spelt out in the song.)

Chicken dinner

Pretty young girl
From the autobiography *Really The Blues*, Mezz Mezzrow and Bernard Wolfe, 1946

Chicken ranch

Brothel

Chicken run

Russian-roulette style race with cars

Chill

1.Kill, assassinate

2. Stop that, wait a minute

Chill your chat

Stop talking

Chime

The time of day, the hour

Chippie

1. Part-time prostitute
"My God! What did I ever think of to put in with a chippy like you?"
From the novel *The High Window*, Raymond Chandler, 1943

See the jazz recording *Chasin' Chippies*, Cootie Williams & his Rug Cutters, 1938

	2. Occasional user of drugs
Chirp	Female vocalist
Chiseler	Swindler, cheat
Chiv	Knife
Choke dog	Rough moonshine liquor
Chop-beatin' session	Discussion
Chop suey	1. A messy death "Some of the nicest people you ever took a gander at suddenly go daffy and make chop suey out of their best friends, with a meat axe." From the film *Sleep, My Love* 2. Having sex See the blues recording *Who'll Chop Your Suey When I'm Gone?*, Willie Jackson, 1926
Chopper	Machine gun, or machine-gunner
Choppers	Teeth
Chops	Any part of the body a musician uses to play his instrument
Chow	Food
Chuck	Food
Chuck horrors	Extreme reaction to food brought on by drug withdrawal
Chump change	Small change, a moderate amount of money, low wages
Cinder dicks	Railroad police
Clam up	Keep quiet, fall silent

Clam yourself	Be quiet, shut up
Clams	Dollars "Nothin' a million clams won't cure." Danny Ocean gets optimistic, from *Ocean's Eleven*, the novelisation of the film screenplay, George Clayton Johnson and Jack Golden Russell, 1960
Claret	Blood
Claws	Fingers
Claws sharp	"The act of being well informed on all subjects." From the booklet *The Jives Of Doctor Hepcat*, Lavada Durst, 1953
Clean	1. Unarmed
	2. Not carrying any stolen goods
Cliff dweller	Resident of a high-rise apartment block
Climb the six-foot ladder	To die, be buried
Clip	1. Kill someone
	2. Punch someone "A guy in the bar come at me with a bottle. I clipped him good, and he busted his head on the bar railing." From the novel *Odds Against Tomorrow*, William P. McGivern, 1957
	3. Cheat someone
Clip joint	Club, bar or other business which routinely swindles its customers
Clipster	Confidence man
Clout	1. Influence, authority
	2. To steal

Clouting heaps	Stealing cars
Clown	Idiot, square, a waste of space
Clued-in	Aware, knowledgeable, on top of the situation
Clutch buster	Hot-rodder
Clyde	A square, a hick, a goon from Straightsville
Coal bin	Blues slang for a vagina "I'll take your order and fill your bin, so get it cleaned out and I'll put it right in, cause I'm just a coal man sellin' the hottest stuff in town." From the blues recording *The Hottest Stuff In Town*, Bob Howe & Frankie Griggs, 1935
Cockroach joint	Cheap restaurant
Coffee grinder	Classic striptease act
Coffin nails	Cigarettes "Get outta here with your coffin nails Can't you see you're on the wrong trail, Go 'way, boy, don't wanna see one lit Or I'll go into a nicotine fit." From the country recording *Nicotine Fit*, Mississippi Slim, 1954
Coffin varnish	Rough liquor
Cold meat cart	Hearse
Cold meat party	A funeral From the novel *Halo In Blood*, Howard Browne, 1946
Cold storage	Prison

| Collar | 1. To arrest someone |
| | 2. To acquire something |

Comb your knowledge box Comb your hair

Combed Searched, frisked
"If a prowl went past, the coppers would comb them sure."
From the novel *Little Men, Big World*, W.R. Burnett, 1951

Come apart like a two-bit suitcase Lose it, fall to pieces, dissolve into tears

Come clean Tell all, speak up, confess
Jazz pioneer Buddy Bolden regularly played a venue in New Orleans around the year 1900 called Come Clean Hall.
"You'd better talk George, come clean. Either you talk, or we'll get it out of the girl."
From the film *The Killing*, 1956

Come to life! Get real, face the truth

Comin' on Hep, in control, confident, like a performer coming onstage and making an entrance

Coney Island whitefish Used condom floating in the sea

Continental A damn, a curse
eg: "I don't give a continental ..."

Cooch dancing Hootchie-cooching, burlesque dancing, stripping

Cook To do something well

Cookie cutter Policeman's badge

Cool 1. In the know, A-ok, hep

2. Unworried, calm, relaxed
See the jazz recording *How You Gonna Keep Kool?*, The Georgia Melodians, 1924
That same year in the Presidential elections, Calvin Coolidge used the slogan "Keep Cool with Coolidge."
See also the jazz recordings *Look Hot, Keep Cool*, The Harmonians, 1933, and *Keep Cool, Fool*, Les Brown & his Orchestra, 1941

Cool, calm and a solid wig

Someone suave, a hepcat, a groover

Cool cat

A dude, a hipster, a real gone daddy
"Ubangi stomp with a rock'n'roll, beats anything that you ever been told. Ubangi stomp, Ubangi style, when it hits it drives a cool cat wild ..."
From the rockabilly recording *Ubangi Stomp*, Warren Smith, 1956

Cool it

Calm down, don't worry, don't make a fuss
"They're ready to fight, but Elmo cuts in, 'Cool it, you studs,' he tells them. 'I said cool it!'"
From the short story *The Rites Of Death*, Hal Ellson, 1956

See also the rock'n'roll song *Cool It, Baby* by Eddie Fontaine, as featured in the 1956 film *The Girl Can't Help It*, which contains the immortal lines:
"I love your eyes, I love your lips, They taste even better than potato chips."

Cooler

Prison cell, solitary confinement

Cop

To obtain

Cop a drear

Die, expire, cash in your chips

Cop a nod	Go to sleep
Cop a plea	Plea bargain in order to get a lower sentence See the jazz recording *Coppin' A Plea*, Gene Krupa & his Orchestra, 1941
Cop a slave	Get a job
Cop a sneak	Surreptitious look
Cop a squat	Sit down
Cop an attitude	Behave in a negative or aggressive fashion
Cop and blow	Easy come, easy go. You win some, you lose some "He reconciled himself to the name of the game. Cop and blow." From the autobiography *I, Paid My Dues*, Babs Gonzales, 1967
Copasetic	Good, in order, everything alright, sometimes spelt copacetic "The highest compliment in the hep world, anything you can do you are a master of it." From the booklet *The Jives Of Doctor Hepcat*, Lavada Durst, 1953
Corn squeezings	Moonshine liquor "Mighty, mighty pleasin' Pappy's corn squeezings, mmm … white lightnin'." From the rockabilly song *White Lightning*, George Jones, 1959
Cornball style	Square, boring, clichéd
Cornfed	From the country, coarse, unsophisticated
Cosmic goo	Metaphysics

"Don't worry me with all that
cosmic goo, I've got practical
problems."
From the novel *Blow Up A Storm*,
Garson Kanin, 1959

County hotel   Local jail

Crack some suds   Drink beer

Crack the books   Read

Crack wise   Joke, talk back, be sarcastic

Crack your jaw   Talk

Crap out   Be unlucky, fail

Crapshoot   A risky business, chancey undertaking

Crash-out   Prison break
Sometimes spoken as crush out. (To
crush, in 19th Century English slang,
meant to run away.)

Crashing the ether   Broadcasting on the radio

Crazy   Good, superlative, wild, the best
"Ooh man, dig those crazy lips
Ooh man, boy she really flips,
Ooh man, dig that crazy chick."
From the R&B jump-jive recording
Dig That Crazy Chick,
Sam Butera & The Witnesses, 1958
See also the rock'n'roll recording
Crazy, Man, Crazy, Bill Haley & The
Comets, 1954

Richard S. Prather, author of numerous
crime novels in the 1950s featuring
private eye Shell Scott, once wrote a
book called *Dig That Crazy Grave*.
During the course of his million-selling
career he also treated the public to *The*

38

Scrambled Yeggs, Have Gat Will Travel
and *The Wailing Frail.*

Crease	1. To shoot "Someone decided to crease Travis. He was shot last night." From the novel *You Can Always Duck*, Peter Cheyney, 1943 2. To hit or to stun
Creep-joint	Brothel where the customers are likely to have their pockets picked
Crib	1. Home, apartment, residence 2. A safe
Croak	Die
Croak sheet	Life insurance policy
Croaker	1. Doctor "'Is Burns bad?' 'Yeah, but the croaker says he'll survive.'" From the novel *The Fast Buck*, James Hadley Chase, 1952 2. Murderer, ie: one who croaks someone
Crocked	Drunk
Croonette	Female singer
Cross-eyed	Drunk
Crowd-pleaser	Police gun
Cruiser	Automobile
Cruising for a bruising	Looking for trouble "Cruising – looking for my gal I'm cruising – goin' don't know where I'm cruising – looking for my gal I'm cruising for a bruising that man with her is gonna get . . ."

	From the rock'n'roll song *Cruising,* Gene Vincent & The Blue Caps, 1956
Cruising with your lights on dim	Stupid, bughouse, not all there
Crumb crushers	Teeth
Crummy	Unpleasant, poor quality, worthless "I sniff at the odour of rotting chow and tell Nick 'Crummy joint.' 'Yeah,' Nick says, 'and crummy people.'" From the novel *Killers Don't Care*, Rod Callahan, 1950
Crunchers	Feet
Cuban candles	Cigars
Cubistic	Square, straight, boring "Mother, you can be such a drag sometimes, so utterly cubistic." From the film *The Young Savages*, 1960
Cupcake	Term of endearment
Current concubine	Girlfriend, steady date
Cut out	Leave, depart
Cut some rug	Dance Pioneer Chicago DJ Jack L.Cooper started a radio show in the early 1930s called *Rug Cutter's Special.* See the blues recording *Rug Cutter Swing*, Henry Allen, 1934
Cut the mustard	Get the job done See the country song *Too Old To Cut The Mustard*, by The Carlisle Brothers, as performed by a teenage Buddy Holly onstage at his school in Lubbock, Texas in 1953, and dedicated to his teachers:

"Used to fight the girls off with a stick, now they say 'He makes me sick.'"

Cut the scene   1. Stop making a fuss

2. Leave, depart

Cutup   Have a laugh, fool around

Cut up rough   Get tough, start a fight

D.O.A.
Dead on arrival, all washed up
"'D.O.A.,' said the intern. 'It looks to me like a stiff dose of cyanide in a cocktail, probably a sidecar.'"
From the short story *Three Wives Too Many*, Kenneth Fearing, 1956

Rudolph Maté directed a film noir called *D.O.A.* in 1950, from a novel by David Goodis (not to be confused with the 1978 documentary film of the Sex Pistols USA tour).

Dabs
Fingerprints

Daddy-O
Term of address for a hipster
New Orleans DJ Vernon Winslow was broadcasting under the name Doctor Daddy-O in the late 1940s. He'd previously called himself Poppa Stoppa. Rock'n'roll DJ Porky Chadwick of WAMO, Pittsburgh called himself "the Daddy-O of the radio, a porkulatin' platter-pushin' Poppa".

Billy Taylor put out a jazz recording in 1955 called *Daddy-O*, and the phrase was also used as the title of one of the great late 1950s exploitation films.

Date bait
Boyfriend or girlfriend

Dame
Woman

Dancing on a dime
Dancing very close together
"Here at the ballroom young men and women come to dance rather than to listen. Preferably on a dime. To sock. In short, to rub bellies together and, thus, excite one another."
From the autobiography *Talking To Myself*, Studs Terkel, 1977

"If you think I'm going dancin' on a dime
your clock is ticking on the wrong time."
Ella Mae Morse to Freddie Slack from the
boogie-woogie recording *House Of Blue
Lights*, 1946

Dangle

Leave, get lost, scram
"Outside, then. Take the air. Dangle."
From the short story *Fly Paper*,
Dashiell Hammett, 1920s

Dead man

Empty bottle

Dead on the vine

Worn out, exhausted

Dead on time

Hep, suave, in the know, on the beam

Dead presidents

Cash money, dollar bills

Dead soldiers

Empty bottles
"Get a load of them dead soldiers. Must
have been some brawl last weekend."
From the film *The Devil Thumbs A
Ride*, 1947

Deadfall

Nightclub or all-night restaurant that is
really a clipjoint

Deal around me

Leave me out of this, I'm not interested

Deep-sea diving

Oral sex
"He's a deep-sea diver
with a stroke that can't go wrong,
he's a deep-sea diver
with a stroke that can't go wrong,
he can touch the bottom
and his wind holds out so long."
From *Empty Bed Blues Part 1*,
Bessie Smith, 1928

Deep six

Dispose of, kill

Delosis

"De-Lo-Sis – a young girl, pretty."
From the booklet *The Jives Of Doctor
Hepcat*, Lavada Durst, 1953

43

Detroit disaster	Automobile
Deuce	Two dollars
Dice-joint	Gambling hall
Dick	Detective "I'm just a square-toed dick. I can't match wits with you." From the novel *The Clue Of The Forgotten Murder*, Erle Stanley Gardner, 1934
Dig	1. Understand, comprehend, appreciate, approve of See the jazz recording *I Don't Dig You Jack*, Blue Lu Barker, 1939 See also the jazz recording *I Dig You The Most*, Kenny Clarke with The Ernie Wilkins Septet, 1955. The flipside was called *Cute Tomato*. 2. To notice, observe or look around "I dug the square for Hassell; he wasn't there, he was in Riker's Island, behind bars." ie: I searched Times Square for him, but he was in jail. From the novel *On The Road*, Jack Kerouac, 1957 3. General word used to punctuate a sentence, to see if your audience is paying attention, dig?
Dig those mellow kicks	Enjoy yourself
Dime	Ten year jail sentence
Dime dropper	Police informer – ie: someone who drops a dime in the payphone to call up the cops
Dime-grind palace	Cheap dancehall with girls available as paid dancing partners

"I work at the Palace Ballroom,
But gee that palace is cheap . . .
Ten cents a dance, pansies and rough guys,
Tough guys who tear my gown."
From the jazz recording *Ten Cents A Dance*, Ruth Etting, 1930

Ding dong daddy
A dude, a hepcat
See the jazz recording *I'm a Ding Dong Daddy (from Dumas)*, Louis Armstrong, 1930 – also recorded by Slatz Randall & his Orchestra, 1930, and the country duo Zeb & Zeke, 1934

Characters in Nelson Algren novels have a habit of singing this song, for instance in *Never Come Morning*, 1941, and *The Man With The Golden Arm*, 1959

Dinner
Pretty young girl
From the autobiography *Really The Blues*, Mezz Mezzrow and Bernard Wolfe, 1946

Dip your bill
Have a drink of booze

Dirty dozens
Trading insults back and forth, each one worse than the last
"'S'pose he tell you he was with you mama.'
'I don't play no dozens, boy,' Smitty growled. 'You young punks don't know how far to go with a man.'"
From the novel *If He Hollers Let Him Go*, Chester Himes, 1945

"Ashes to ashes, sand to sand,
I like your mama but she got too many men . . ."
From the blues recording *The Dirty Dozens*, Speckled Red, 1930

Dirty with money
Rolling in it, rich, wealthy

Dish
Good looking person

45

"You're a swell dish. I think I'm gonna go for you."
Jimmy Cagney in the film *The Public Enemy*, 1933

Dish it out
Hand something out: punishment, information, etc
See the jazz recording *I Can Dish It, Can You Take It*, Blue Scott & his Blue Boys, 1936

Dish the dirt
Tell the story, give away secrets

Disk
Record, platter, waxing, a solid slab of sound
In the late fifties, *Mad* magazine did a parody of all the current rock'n'roll fan magazines and called it *Diskville*, which claimed "Frankie Avalon's new record is called *My Teenage Lips Are Chapped From Kissing An Ice Cold Chick*."

Dissolve
Leave in a hurry, disappear

Dixie fried
Drunk
Dixie, as well as being the traditional name for the Southern states, is also one of the most popular brands of beer in the region.
"He hollered 'Rave on, children, I'm with ya,
Rave on, cats' he cried.
'It's almost dawn and the cops are gone
Lets all get dixie fried ...'"
From the rockabilly recording *Dixie Fried*, Carl Perkins, 1956

Do a Houdini
Disappear, leave in a hurry

Do a number on someone
Pull the wool over their eyes, deceive, con

Do right man
Someone who plays it straight, who wouldn't cheat on their partner

See the blues recording *Do Right Papa*, Butterbeans & Susie, 1925; the western swing recording *I'm A Do Right Papa,* Leon's Lone Star Cowboys, 1935; the country recording *I'm a Do Right Cowboy*, Tex Ritter, 1935

Dog around

1. Nag, verbally abuse
"Give me a break, Papa,
don't throw your sweet mama down.
You've treated me so mean,
ain't you tired of doggin' me round?"
From the blues recording *Give Me a Break Blues*, Ida Cox, 1927
See also the blues recording *If You Don't Want Me (Stop Doggin' Me Round)*, Jan Garber, 1924

2. Following someone
"Who's the ugly lob at the end of the bar chilling us? He's dogging me. Doesn't seem to care if I know it or not."
From the novel *Darling, It's Death*, Richard S. Prather, 1953

Doghouse

Double bass
"The car radio gave me 'Whispers', very softly, with a lot of strings, a growling doghouse and a sobbing trumpet."
From the novel *Halo In Blood*, Howard Browne, 1946

Dogs

Feet
"Keep your dog on it. "
ie: Keep your foot on the accelerator.
From the novel *Red Harvest*, Dashiell Hammett, 1929

See the blues recording *Got To Cool My Doggies Now,* Mamie Smith & her Jazz Hounds, 1922

Doing it all

Serving a life sentence in jail

47

Doing next week's drinking too soon	Those extra shots of booze that you really don't need because you're totally plastered already
Doing the book	Serving a life sentence in jail "'He told me to tell you not to worry about him.' 'He's doing the book, I worry plenty.' 'Well, he's a tough kid, maybe he'll get a break.'" From the film *The Killing*, 1956
Doll	Good looking girl "It was a woman, a doll, a sensational tomato who looked as if she'd just turned twenty-one, but had obviously signalled for the turn a long time ago. She was tall, and lovely all over, maybe five-seven, and she wore a V-necked white blouse, as if she were the gal who'd invented cleavage just for fun." From the novel *Always Leave 'Em Dying*, Richard S. Prather, 1961
Dollface	Term of endearment
Domino	To stop, to finish
Don't get your gauge up	Don't get excited, calm down
Don't let the grass grow in your ears	To be lazy or otherwise untogether
Don't let your mouth start something your head can't stand	Shut up or I'll hit you
Don't move a peg	Stay still "When I say stop, don't move a peg ..." From the piano boogie recording *Pine Top's Boogie Woogie*, Pine Top Smith, 1928

48

Don't raise no needless dust	Don't make a fuss, don't go out of your way
Don't strip your gears	Be cool, don't blow your top
Don't sweat it	Don't worry about it
Don't take any wooden nickels	Be careful, watch your step See the jazz recording *'Tain't Good (Like a Nickel Made of Wood)*, Jimmy Lunceford & his Orchestra, 1936
Don't vip another vop	Don't say another word
Dope	1. Heroin 2. Information eg: "What's the dope?"
Dope it out	Reason things out, explain "I tried to dope it out, a screwy thing like that. I added up and subtracted and tried to remember back to certain times and places, and all I got out of it was a headache." From the novel *Savage Night*, Jim Thompson, 1953
Double-barrelled shotgun	Harmonica that can be played from both sides
Dough	Money "Plenty tough boy, and rolling in dough. Always had a bankroll that would choke a mule." From the novel *Little Men, Big World*, W.R. Burnett, 1951 See the jazz recording *What'll We Do For Dough?*, Walter Anderson & his Golden Pheasant Hoodlums, 1927
Doughnut	1. Automobile tyre

2. Blues slang for vagina
See the blues recordings *Mama's
Doughnut*, Spark Plug Smith, 1933,
and *Who Pumped The Wind In My
Doughnut?*, Washboard Sam, 1935

Douse the Edisons   1. Put the lights out

2. Close your eyes

Douse the glim   Put the lights out

Down with the fish   Drunk

Drag   1. A bringdown, something depressing

2. Influence
eg: "He's got a lot of drag with the politi-
cians downtown."

3. "Fun, killer, swinger, dumb."
From the booklet *The Jives Of Doctor
Hepcat*, Lavada Durst, 1953

4. Dance
"Nothing braces me up like a good drag
across the slag with a hag ..."
Charming sentiments from the film
Shake, Rattle And Rock, 1957

Drag-and-eat pad   Restaurant

Draggin'-wagon   A hot car, something really fast
"He wanted to get out of the two-wheel
class and own a draggin' wagon."
From the novel *Go, Man, Go!*,
Edward De Roo, 1959

**Dragging your
rear axle**   Beating about the bush, prevaricating
"Come to the point, you're dragging
your rear axle in waltz-time."
From the film *High School Confidential*,
1958

Dragnet

Major police search, city- or even countrywide
"'Are you throwing out a dragnet?'
'Sorry, no dragnet Charlie. We've got a book full of names, addresses and phone numbers to check.'"
From the film *Side Street*, 1950

Drape

1. A suit of clothes

2. "To dress or to lounge."
From the booklet *The Jives Of Doctor Hepcat*, Lavada Durst, 1953

Draw a lot of water

To have a lot of influence

Draw one

I'd like a coffee

Draw one in the dark

I'd like a black coffee

Drift

Get lost, go away, leave
"'Beat it,' he said. 'Drift. Take the air. Scram. Push off.'"
From the novel *The High Window*, Raymond Chandler, 1943

Drill

Shoot someone

Drilling

To walk, to move in a straight line

Drinking that mess

Tipping it back, sucking the bottle
"Drinking that mess is pure delight,
when they get drunk they start fighting all night,
kicking out windows and knocking down doors,
drink a half a gallon and holler for more . . ."
From the R&B recording
Drinkin' Wine Spo-Dee-O-Dee,
Stick McGhee, 1949

Drinking the town dry

A wild night, hitting the bottle high

Drinking your lunch out of a bottle   Being an alcoholic

Driving   Having sex
"I've been driving fourteen years,
haven't had an accident yet . . ."
From *Henry Ford Blues*,
Roosevelt Sykes, 1929

See the blues recordings *Hard Driving
Papa*, Bessie Smith, 1926,
and *Hitch Me To Your Buggy,
And Drive Me Like a Mule,*
Casey Bill Weldon, 1927

Drop that back into low and go by once more   Can you say that again please

Drop the veil   Stop pretending and come clean
"Drop the veil, sister, I'm in the business
myself."
From the film *The Big Sleep,* 1946

Drugstore cowboy   Young loafer on the streetcorner

Drunk tank   Holding cell for prisoners brought in
drunk

Dryer than a cork leg   Thirsty, in need of some booze

Duck soup   In the writings of Dashiell Hammett this
means a sure thing, something
very easily accomplished.
However, Nelson Algren uses it to mean
something strange and not quite as it
should be:
"'I hope he knows what he's doin' is all,'
Mama T. observed dubiously. 'It looked
queer as duck soup to me.'"
From the novel *Never Come Morning*,
Nelson Algren, 1941
For the Marx Brothers, it meant whatever
the hell they wanted it to mean . . .

Dude

1. A suave cat, a hipster, well dressed
The U.S. Phonograph Company issued a wax cylinder in the early 1890s by Russell Hunting called *Casey And The Dude In A Street Car*.

Raoul Whitfield wrote a story called *Sal The Dude* for the October 1929 issue of *Black Mask* magazine.

2. Guy, man, fella

Duded up

Well dressed, sharp

Duds

Clothes

Duked out

Dressed up, well turned out
"He was all duked out in a hard-boiled collar and a blue serge suit. There was a hatchet-faced dame with him in a stiff black satin dress and a hat that looked like a lamp shade."
From the novel *Savage Night*, Jim Thompson, 1953

Dukes

Fists
"'You know how to handle your dukes, man,' he said. 'Shortest fight we've had around here yet.'"
From the short story *A Hood Is Born*, Richard Deming, 1959

Dumb gat

A gun fitted with a silencer

Dummy-up

Fall silent, refuse to talk

Dump

Dwelling, building, apartment. It can be in any condition from well preserved to falling down. The phrase "Nice dump you've got here" is intended as a compliment, not an insult

Dungaree doll

Hip girl wearing jeans
"The flat top cats and the dungaree dolls

Are headed for the gym to the sock-hop ball,
The joint's really jumpin', the cats are going wild,
The music really sends me, I dig the crazy styles."
From the rock'n'roll recording *Ready Teddy*, Little Richard, 1956

Dust

1. Kill

2. Leave, depart
"Get moving: we may have to dust, and dust fast!"
From the novel *The Fast Buck*,
James Hadley Chase, 1952

Dustin' the keys

Playing piano

Dutch milk

Beer

The eagle flies on Friday — Getting paid

Early bright — The early hours of the morning

Easy rider — Good at sex
See the blues recording *I Wonder Where My Easy Rider's Gone,* Tampa Red & his Hokum Jug Band, 1929
See also the blues recordings *Ride, Jockey, Ride*, Trixie Smith & her Down Home Syncopators, 1924 (billed as "exciting enough to stir up a dead man"); *Rider Needs A Fast Horse*, Ora Alexander, 1931; *Easy Ridin' Mama*, Washboard Sam, 1937; and the vocal group recording *I'm Gonna Ride Tillie Tonight*, The Fortunes, 1948

Eat crow — Be humiliated, forced to apologise

Eat your mush and hush — Shut up and eat your food

Eats factory — Restaurant

Edisons — 1. Eyes

2. Lights

Eggs in the dark — Eggs fried on both sides

Eighty-eight — Oldsmobile 88, a car from the early 1950s also known as a Rocket 88
"Got me a date and I won't be late, Pick her up in my eighty-eight."
From the rock'n'roll recording *Rip It Up*, Little Richard, 1956
See also the rock'n'roll recording *Rocket 88*, Jackie Brenston & his Delta Cats, 1951

Eighty-eights	Piano
Eighty-six	Ditch, dispose of, drop
Electric cure	The electric chair "Ned Beaumont smiled tepidly and asked with mock admiration: 'Is there anything you haven't been through before? Ever been given the electric cure?'" From the novel *The Glass Key*, Dashiell Hammett, 1931
Elephant teeth	Piano keys "The cat that's pulling the elephant teeth is a bonnet-flipper and makes a gang of mad beats." ie: He's a damned good piano player. From the booklet *The Jives Of Doctor Hepcat*, Lavada Durst, 1953
Elevated	Drunk, high
Embalmed	Drunk, loaded
Embalmer	Bootlegger
Embalming fluid	Alcohol
Empty enough to steal the dog's dinner	Hungry
Enamel	Skin From the autobiography *Really The Blues*, Mezz Mezzrow and Bernard Wolfe, 1946
Enough bread to burn a wet mule	Very rich From the autobiography *I, Paid My Dues*, Babs Gonzales, 1967
Equalizer	Gun
Eternal checkout	Death

Evaporate	Leave, depart, say goodbye
Evening rig	Formal dress, dinner jacket, black tie etc
Every-which-way drunk	Catatonic, totally plastered, drinking yourself insensible "I was taken drunk that year – every-which-way drunk . . ." From the short story *The Lost Decade*, F. Scott Fitzgerald, 1939
Everything is much straight	Things are fine, mellow, A-ok
Everything plus	Good-looking, the works eg: "She was a swell dame with everything plus."
Exectutive session	Serious drinking "I remembered the half bottle of scotch I had left and went into executive session with it." Philip Marlowe in the short story *Trouble Is My Business*, Raymond Chander, 1939
Eyeballing	Looking at, observing "For once no-one was looking at Trammell; all ten thousand or so were eyeballing me." From the novel *Always Leave 'Em Dying*, Richard S. Prather, 1961

Face like the elevated railway	Ugly
Face like a Russian flag	Embarrassed
Fade out	Leave, often in a hurry
Fair shake	A decent chance, an equal opportunity
Fall down, juvenile	Stop bothering me, you irritating youth From the film *Beat Girl*, 1960
Fall guy	One who takes the blame for something, sometimes an innocent party "'They got me measured for the fall guy.' 'Now just a minute ...' 'Sure, I'm the fortune hunter that hypnotised Marsha, who made her kill her father for his money.'" From the film *Touch Of Evil*, 1959
Fall in	Arrive
Fall out	1. Depart 2. Go to sleep
Fall in and dig the happenings	Come on in and have a good time, listen to this
Fan	Pick someone's pocket
Fan someone's baggage	Search their belongings "I'm clean. Go ahead, fan me, c'mon ..." From the film *Pickup On South Street*, 1953
Far out	1. Weird 2. Impressive

58

Feeling no pain	Drunk, high, loaded See the jazz recording *Feelin' No Pain*, The Charleston Chasers, 1927
Fess up	Speak up, give out some information, confess
Filling station	Bar or off-licence
Fin	Five dollar bill
Fine as wine	Good, the best "They say it's fine as wine and really on the ball, No windows, no doors, it's just a hole in the wall." Amos Milburn describes his ideal night- club, from the boogie-woogie recording *Chicken Shack Boogie*, 1946
Fine frame, no parts lame	Good looking, having a good figure
Fink	Informer, stool pigeon
Finger-man	Someone who sets up another person, either for arrest or assassination – puts the finger on them Raymond Chandler published a short story called *Finger Man* in the October 1934 issue of *Black Mask* magazine "They killed the Mover and they killed Anna, and they tried to kill me. They are now in bad trouble. I want the finger man. As soon as I figure out who he is, he's dead." From the novel *Little Men, Big World*, W.R. Burnett, 1951 "I picked up the guy in a flea-bag hotel on Doncelos – his doll fingered him – and picked up the swag with him." From the novel *Darling, It's Death*, Richard S. Prather, 1959

Fish	1. A sucker, a rube
	2. A dollar
Fish wrapper	A newspaper
Fishtail	Movement of car where the rear end swings from side to side
Flake	Unreliable, no good, a waste of space
Flap your ears	Listen "Go right ahead baby, my ears are flappin'." From the novel *Your Deal, My Lovely*, Peter Cheyney, 1941
Flash your welcome sign	Give me some encouragement "Your lips start me to burnin' with a desire an' a yearnin', to feel them cling to mine, well if you're with me flash your welcome sign." From *Are You With Me*, Mel Robbins, 1956
Flat as a matzoh	Broke, out of cash
Flat on your can	Down on your luck
Flat tyre	1. A letdown
	2. Impotent "Couple of lightweights . . . yeah, flat tyres." Joan Blondell talking about the men she's with, who've both passed out from drink. From the film *The Public Enemy*, 1933
Fleabag	Cheap rooming house or hotel
Flimflam	Deception, con, swindle
Flip	Go wild, get excited, real gone "I flipped my lid

I blew my top,
When I got roarin'
On a real cool bop ..."
From the rock'n'roll recording *I Flipped,*
Gene Vincent & The Blue Caps, 1956

Flip your wig   1. Jump for joy, bust a gasket

2. Go insane, lose your cool
"I figured she was the type to flip good
if she flipped."
From the novel *Always Leave 'Em
Dying*, Richard S. Prather, 1961

Flippy   Really good, excellent, the most
"'Doll, where have you been?'
'Right in your little heart, Doll.'
'You didn't say a thing about my outfit.'
'Flippy ... real flippy.'"
Elvis charms his date, from the film
Jailhouse Rock, 1957

Floating   Drunk
"I poured her a slug that would have
made me float over a wall."
From the novel *Farewell, My Lovely*,
Raymond Chandler, 1940

Floozie   Tart, dancehall doll, streetwalker

Floozie-joint   Whorehouse

Flophouse   Cheap rooms, doss house

Florida honeymoon   A dirty weekend, a holiday affair

Fly   Smart, sophisticated, in the know
From the autobiography *Really The
Blues*, Mezz Mezzrow and Bernard Wolfe,
1946
In England in the early 19th century, the
word was already in use as a term for
someone who understood the latest slang.

See the jazz recording *I Ain't Your Hen,
Mr. Fly Rooster*, Martha Copeland, 1928

61

Fly it through to endsville	Bring it to a conclusion
Fly the coop	Leave, often in a hurry. Leave home
Foam	Beer
Focus your audio	Listen carefully
Fogged	Killed, rubbed out "The smooth-faced young man had his pistol out again. 'I can fog him easy, Slats,' he said." From the novel *Red Gardenias*, Jonathan Latimer, 1939
Foggy	"Full, crowded, loaded." From the booklet *The Jives Of Doctor Hepcat*, Lavada Durst, 1953
Folding green	Banknotes "Just put this hunk of the folding green back in your saddle bag and forget you ever met me." From the novel *The Little Sister*, Raymond Chandler, 1949
For you and me the chill is on	Our relationship is over
Foul-up	A mistake
Four-flushing	Cheating, lying, untrustworthy ". . . this goddam four-flushing town, all the viciousness and cruelty." Horace McCoy praises good old Hollywood, from the novel *I Should Have Stayed Home*, 1938 See the blues recording *Four Flushing Papa (You've Gotta Play Straight With Me)*, Lillian Goodner & her Sawin' Trio, 1924

A film called *The Four Flusher* starring
Marion Nelson and George Lewis played
the American theatre circuit in 1928.

**Fracture your
toupee**

Go crazy

Fractured

1. Drunk

2. Real gone, blown away, excited
"I'm fractured! fractured!
that music fractures me ..."
From the rock'n'roll recording *Fractured*,
Bill Haley & The Comets, 1953

Frail

Dame, doll, sweetheart, mainsqueeze
Eric Howard wrote a story called *The
Fifty Grand Frail* for the November
1938 issue of *Black Mask* magazine.

"She was the roughest, toughest frail, but
Minnie had a heart as big as a whale."
From the jazz recording *Minnie The
Moocher*, Cab Calloway & his Orchestra,
1931

See also *The Wailing Frail*, a late 1950s
novel by Richard S. Prather

Frantic threads

Hip clothes, sharp apparel

Freak

A fan of something, an enthusiast
eg: a hotrod freak

Fresh fish special

Bad prison haircut given to recent arrivals
– the fresh fish
"What about your haircut? Do you want a
good one or do you want a fresh fish
special – they hack it up. A good one'll
cost you three packets of cigarettes."
From the film *Jailhouse Rock*, 1957

Fried

1. Given the electric chair

2. Drunk or high on drugs

Fried, dyed and swept to the side	Having your hair done, the full treatment, having it straightened, coloured and set
Friend of boys on the loose	Good-time girl, of the kind that frequently seem to show up in Mickey Spillane novels "She was a taxi-dancer, a night club entertainer, friend of boys on the loose and anything else you can mention where sex is concerned." From the novel *Kiss Me, Deadly*, 1953
Friends in the bank	Money "I've got a nice little joint at the Ambassador, with a built-in bar; I've got a swell bunch of telephone numbers and several thousand friends in the bank." From the novel *Fast One*, Paul Cain, 1936
Frill	Girl, dame – similar to frail "Half the guys in Hollywood was tryin' to marry this frill ... the other half already had." From the novel *You Can Always Duck,* Peter Cheyney, 1943
From soup to nuts	Everything, the whole shooting match Felix Arndt released a ragtime record in 1914 called *From Soup to Nuts*.
Fronts	"Clothes, suits, money." From the booklet *The Jives Of Doctor Hepcat,* Lavada Durst, 1953
Fruitcake	Crazy person, weirdo
Fumigate your brains	Smoke a cigarette
Funky	Smelly, obnoxious From the autobiography *Really The Blues*, Mezz Mezzrow and Bernard Wolfe, 1946

Kenna's Hall, a New Orleans jazz hang-out on Perdido Street, which was Buddy Bolden's regular gig venue in 1900, was known to everyone as Funky Butt Hall, or F.B. Hall for short.

See also *Ain't Love Grand (Don't Get Funky)*, a jazz recording by John Hyman's Bayou Stompers, 1927

In 1950s jazz circles the word was quite common, for instance *Funk Junction* by King Pleasure & The Quincy Jones Band, 1954, or *Creme de Funk* by Phil Woods and Gene Quill, 1957. That same year, the Gene Ammons' Allstars put out an album called *Funky*.

Funnel   A heavy drinker

Fusebox   Head

G

G   One thousand dollars, a grand

G.I. Blues   Morbid fear of being in the army
"'He been reading in the paper where all the young men gonna be called to the Army,' Peaches said. 'He got the GI Blues.'"
From the novel *If He Hollers Let Him Go*, Chester Himes, 1945

See also the jazz recording *Desperate G.I. Blues*, Cousin Jo with Pete Brown's Blue Blowers, 1946

G-man   Government agent, the Feds, the FBI
Dwight V. Babcock wrote a story for the January 1936 issue of *Black Mask* magazine called *'G-Man' Chuck Thompson*

See the jazz recording *G-Men*, Cootie Williams & his Orchestra, 1941

Gabber   Radio commentator or D.J.

Gabfest   Argument, conversation

Gams   Legs
When Mildred Pierce hits the headlines, a press photographer yells at her in an effort to get a little more leg in the picture: "The gams, the gams! Your face ain't news."
From the novel *Mildred Pierce*, James M. Cain, 1943

Gargle   Drink

Gargle factory   Bar, alehouse

Gas   1. To talk

2. Something really good

Gasser

Something or someone that takes your breath away
From the autobiography *Really The Blues*, Mezz Mezzrow and Bernard Wolfe, 1946

"I copped a gig at Mintons and one night Alfred Lions came in to dig us. He said we gassed him, but we were too far out for the people."
From the autobiography *I, Paid My Dues*, Babs Gonzales, 1967

See the jazz recording *That's A Gasser*, Wingy Manone, 1945

"'Hey gasser, you lookin' for me?'
'Fall down, juvenile . . .'"
From the film *Beat Girl*, 1960

Gassing the slobs

Impressing your audience

Gassing your moss

Getting your hair straightened

Gat

Gun
"You know, you're the second guy I've met today that seems to think a gat in the hand means the world by the tail."
Humphrey Bogart in the film version of *The Big Sleep*, 1946

Gate

Hipster greeting for a fellow dude, short for *gate mouth*
In 1926 Columbia Records issued a record called *Gate Mouth* by The New Orleans Wanderers with an advert that read "Gate Mouth swings wide and handsome . . . this is the kind of mouth that stretches from ear to ear and buttons in the back".

Down Beat's 1939 Yearbook of Swing defined Gate as a "Word of greeting between musicians."

See the jazz recording *Stomp It Out, Gate*, Rosetta Howard & The Harlem Hamfats, 1938

Gator

In 1953 Doctor Hepcat wrote that the word gator was interchangable with the word cat

"The old jukebox was blowin' out the beat
The cats and the gators were shakin' their feet."
From the rockabilly recording *Three Alley Cats*, Roy Hall, 1955

Geek

1. Lowest type of carnival sideshow performer, often featured in a cage, biting the heads off live chickens

2. Awkward person, weird looking

Geets

Money
See the vocal group recording
All *My Geets Are Gone*,
The Five Blazes, 1947

In *Carny Kill*, a 1966 crime novel by Robert Edmond Alter, the word is spelt slightly differently: "I got enough geetus that I don't have to live up here if I don't want."

Gentle up a drink

Add some more alcohol to the mixture, make it more potent

Germsville

A hospital

Get a glow

Get drunk

Get both your eyes wet

Get drunk

Get in the wind

To leave

Get off the fence, Hortense

Make a decision, say what you mean

Get out of your fighting clothes and come to earth	Don't take offence so easily, calm down From the novel *Little Caesar*, W.R. Burnett, 1929
Get my bread or I take your head	Babs Gonzales' time-honoured phrase designed to persuade club owners to pay his band at the end of the evening From the autobiography *I, Paid My Dues*, 1967
Get the blast put on you	Getting shot, having someone drill you a new navel "Occasionally someone got the blast put on him – but only as a last resort." From the novel *Little Men, Big World*, W.R.Burnett, 1951
Get wise	Understand, learn something
Get with it	1. Be where it's at, make the scene, be aware "We're gonna have a downbeat We're gonna have a ball, Get 'em on their feet Gonna rock 'em all, But we gotta get with it 'Fore the night is gone." From the rockabilly recording *Get With It*, Charlie Feathers, 1956 See also the jazz recording *Git Wid It*, Paul Martell Orchestra, 1944 2. Have sex "Let's get with it, please baby ..." From the novel *Go, Man, Go!*, Edward De Roo, 1959
Get your hambone boiled	Have sex "I'm going to Washington to get my hambone boiled, 'cause these men in Atlanta bound to let my hambone spoil." From the blues recording *Nothin' But*

	Blues, Cleo Gibson & her Hot Three, 1929
Get your kicks	Have a wild time, become excited, enjoy yourself "Get your kicks on Route 66." From the R&B recording *Route 66*, Roy Brown, 1946
Getting mighty crowded	Under pressure, tense
Getting the shakes	Becoming afraid, agitated, worked up
Gig	1. Musical engagement
	2. Any job or occupation
Giggle water	Alcohol
Gimme some skin	Hipster handshake See the jazz recording *Give Me Some Skin*, Lionel Hampton & his Sextet, 1941
	"Now gimme some skin, and ooze it out ..." From the film *The Wild One*, 1954
Gimp	Lame, someone who walks with a limp eg: Moe The Gimp, 1920s mobster who married singer Ruth Etting.
Ginhead	A drunk, an alcoholic
Ginmill	Bar, saloon, taproom, speakeasy "One of the best Race releases is Okeh 8747, whereon the Hokum Boys discourse in haphazard and lighthearted fashion on the *Folks Down South* and the *Gin Mill Blues* ..." From the magazine *Phonograph Monthly Review*, New York, February 1930
Ginmill cowboys	Bar regulars, bottle babies

Ginmill perfume	Alcohol breath
Gin palace	Bar
Give him a permanent wave	To send someone to the electric chair
Give him the air	Tell him goodbye, finish the relationship, ignore him "Dorothy Brock don't mean that to me. If it hadn't have been for me, she wouldn't have had a show to star in. She'd better not try to give me the air now." From the film *42nd Street*, 1933
Give him the heat	To shoot someone From the novel *Dames Don't Care*, Peter Cheyney, 1937
Give him the works	Shoot him "So you didn't try to make a deal before giving him the works?" From the film *The Maltese Falcon*, 1941
Give it the gas	Step on it, get moving "You can jump in my Ford and give her the gas, Pull out the throttle, don't give me no sass, Take your foot, slap it on the floor, When you get here we'll rock some more . . ." From the rock'n'roll recording *End Of The Road*, Jerry Lee Lewis, 1956 "A detective jumps in my cab and says 'Follow that black sedan, it's full of thieves.' So I give her the gas . . ." From the film *Where The Sidewalk Ends*, 1950
Give it the go-by	Pass up the opportunity, decline

Give me an intro to this snake and I'll hitch up the reindeers for you	Introduce me to this despicable person and I'll get the marijuana cigarettes for you to smoke From the film *High School Confidential*, 1958
Give out	1. Speak up, tell all, come across 2. Play music from the heart
Give the gate	Send someone away, fire them, send them packing "I wondered whether there wasn't some safe way of getting Fay to give her the gate." ie: Couldn't Fay find an excuse to sack her? From the novel *Savage Night*, Jim Thompson, 1953
Give the glad eye	Leer at, flirt with, look over "'He doesn't look like a shamus,' he says. 'I've seen him trying to toss Ava the glad eye. He acts more like a hood on the loose.'" From the novel *Killers Don't Care*, Rod Callahan, 1950
Give the hurry call	Telling someone to get here fast, get a move on
Give the place the broom	Search the building
Glass or a funnel?	How would you like your drink?
Glasses	"She's a remarkable lady, she's seventy-four years old and she don't need glasses. She drinks right out of the bottle, this cat . . ." Dean Martin onstage at The Sands, Las Vegas, February 1964
Glom	1. Acquire, obtain, steal Dashiell Hammett in his novel *The Dain Curse*, 1928, spells it slightly differently:

"Looks like him and
another guy glaumed the ice ..."

2. Observe, look at

Gobble pipe   Saxophone

Go, cat, go!   Exclamation of encouragement, hipster-style
"One for the money,
two for the show,
three to get ready
now go, cat, go ..."
From *Blue Suede Shoes*, Carl Perkins,
1956

See also the novel *Go, Cat, Go!*,
Edward de Roo, 1959

**Go home and
wrastle with that
one**   That's what I can do – see if you can
do better

**Go into your
dance, buddy**   Alright, let's hear it, speak your
piece

**Go on a deep six
holiday**   To be buried, to die

**Go pick yourself
an orchid**   Get lost, scram

Go press the bricks   Take a walk, get lost

**Go the whole
bundle**   Take a chance

**Go to a museum
for your art lessons**   Stop leering at me

**God sure don't
like ugly**   You get what's coming to you
From the autobiography *Really The
Blues*, Mezz Mezzrow and Bernard Wolfe,
1946

"I don't tell nothin' but the truth, because God don't like ugly."
From the novel *A Hearse of Another Colour*, M.E.Chaber, 1959

Going commercial

Becoming a prostitute, selling it on the street

Going rotary

Blowing your top, losing it, going wild

Going steady with Mary Jane

Having a marijuana habit

Going to fist city

Going to have a fight

Going to hell in a handbasket

Turning bad, going to waste, going down the tubes
"Did that explain why I'm all mixed up? Why I'm a no-good bum ... why I'm a delinquent slob going to hell in a handbasket?"
From the novel *Savage Streets*, William P. McGivern, 1959

Going to slice city

Going to cut somebody up

Gold

Money

Gold digger

Someone looking for a rich partner
From the novel *Gentlemen Prefer Blondes*, Anita Loos, 1926

See also the film *Gold Diggers of 1933*, 1933

Goldfish room

Police interrogation room, usually fitted with a one-way glass for observation purposes

Gone

Out of this world, superlative
"I have found the gonest little girl in the world and I am going straight to the Lion's Den with her tonight."
From the novel *On The Road*, Jack Kerouac, 1957

74

"Gee Vince, when you sing, it's really Gonesville."
Vince Everett (Elvis Presley) makes a big impression on a fan, from the film *Jailhouse Rock*, 1957

Gone with the gin   Drunk, out of it, plastered
See the jazz recording *Gone With The Gin*, Hot Lips Page & his Band, 1940

Good-gal   Girlfriend
"My good-gal loves me,
everybody knows,
and she paid a hundred cash dollars,
just bought me a suit of clothes."
From the country recording *Blue Yodel No. 9*, Jimmie Rodgers, 1930

Good sauce from the gravy bowl   Alcohol
"We used to call booze 'sauce' and the gravy bowl was a cup."
From the autobiography *Of Minnie The Moocher And Me*, Cab Calloway, 1976

The goods   Good looking
"This dame is certainly the goods."
From the novel *Dames Don't Care,* Peter Cheyney, 1937

Goo-goo eyes and wolf whistles   Leering appreciation

Goof   Mistake, error
Satirising the writers of *Playboy* magazine in the early 1960s, the Reverend Roy Larsen came up with the following:
"Give us this day our daily Martinis
– dry and smooth – and forgive us our goofs, even as we overlook the goofs of others . . ."

Goon from Saskatoon   An idiot, a square

Gorilla   Tough guy, mobster, strong-arm boy

"The two gorillas yank him to his feet and Merilli slugs him again. This time hard in the guts."
From the novel *Killers Don't Care*, Rod Callahan, 1950

Got it made in the shade
It's done, taken care of, I've got what I wanted

Gouge
1. Obtain
"I gouged twenty dollars out of her for expenses."
Philip Marlowe in the short story *Trouble Is My Business*, Raymond Chandler, 1939

2. Swindle or cheat

Grab a flop
Sit down, have a chair

Grab some air
Put your hands up, I have a gun

Grabbers
Hands

Grandstanding
Showing off

Grape cat
Wino

Grass
Marijuana

Grasshopper
Marijuana smoker, weedhead

Graveyard shift
Night work

Gravy
1. Money
"Maybe the Guardians wanted the gravy, or the glory, or maybe Trammell was just too damned stinking to live – but they knocked their boy off."
From the novel *Always Leave 'Em Dying*, Richard S. Prather, 1961

2. Sexual fluids
See *You Can Dip Your Bread In My Gravy, But You Can't Have None Of My*

Chops, a shy retiring blues recording from 1925 by Virginia Liston. The previous year she released a song called *You've Got The Right Key, But The Wrong Keyhole.*

3. Something easy
eg: "It wasn't all gravy."

Graze on some grass
Smoke the weed
From the film *High School Confidential*, 1958

Grease
1. Protection money or a bribe

2. Sexual fluids
See the blues recordings *I Want Plenty Grease In My Frying Pan*, Margaret Carter, 1926; *Fat Greasy Baby,* Robert Peeples, 1930; *Take It Easy, Greasy,* Lil Johnson, 1936

Grease joint
Cheap restaurant

Grease monkey
Mechanic

Grease your chops
Eat

Greased
1. Killed

2. Drunk

Greenbacks
Dollars

Greetings, gate, let's dissipate
The proper salutation when meeting a fellow hepster at the bar, according to Cab Calloway's Swingformation Bureau.

Grift
A racket, swindle or other illegal means of making a few bucks, not usually involving violence

Grifter
Cheap crook, swindler
"By the time she was twenty-one in 1926, she definitely preferred Tenth

Avenue to Fifth, grifters to bankers, and Hymie the Riveter to the Honourable Cecil Windown, who had asked her to marry him."
From the short story *Fly Paper*, Dashiell Hammett, 1920s

Probably the most famous use of the word came in 1963, when Jim Thompson published his novel *The Grifters*.

Grind   Striptease performance

Grind house   Striptease joint, or cheap cinema

Grinding   1. Slow, sexy dancing
"This is a real slow number playing, and one thing about China. She know how to do like a snake with them slow discs. I'm all for that, and we do some slow grinding."
From the short story *The Rites Of Death,* Hal Ellson, 1956

2. Having sex
In his 1957 novel *A Walk On The Wild Side*, two of Nelson Algren's characters flirt with each other by discussing coffee grinding in a suggestive manner:
"'It's always best do you grind your own, miss. For that way it's much fresher.'
'So you say. But what good is fresh if there ain't enough to satisfy? Mister, if you talkin' 'bout some little old scrawny-size pot I ain't interested. What I needs is a great big pot, enough for both morning and night.'
'So long as it make good cawfee, miss, size don't scarcely matter ...'"

"Bought me a coffee grinder,
the best that I could find,
bought me a coffee grinder,
the best that I could find,

Lord he can grind my coffee
cause he has a brand new grind."
From the blues recording *Empty Bed
Blues Part 1,* Bessie Smith, 1928

See also the blues recordings
*Ain't Got Nobody to Grind My Coffee,
(b/w Take Your Finger Off It),* Mary
Stafford, 1926; *Organ Grinder Blues,*
Victoria Spivey, 1928; *My Georgia
Grind,* Lucille Bogan, 1930; *Steady
Grindin',* James "Stump" Johnson, 1933

Grinding mill

1. Machine gun on tripod
"Tell him to set up his mill and start
grinding."
From the novel *Red Harvest,*
Dashiell Hammett, 1929

2. Vagina
"She grinds my meal in the morning,
and she grinds it late at night,
she grinds my meal in the morning,
and she grinds it late at night,
she grinds it in a way
suit any man's appetite."
From the blues recording *Grinding Mill,*
Johnny Temple, 1939

Groan box

Accordian

Groghound

Drunkard, alcoholic

Groove a tune

Cut a record, lay down some tracks, wax
a platter
"We grooved a couple of tunes in
New York and caught a wire at a
nitery here in Chicago."
ie: We recorded a couple of songs and
then got a contract to broadcast from a
nightclub.
From the novel *The Lady in the
Morgue,* Jonathan Latimer, 1936

Groover

Someone righteous, hep, solid, on the
square

79

Groovy

"Really good, in the groove, enjoyable."
From the autobiography *Really The Blues*, Mezz Mezzrow and Bernard Wolfe, 1946

"'I decided at the last moment that I couldn't live without you'
'You sound groovy ...'"
From the novel *If He Hollers Let Him Go*, Chester Himes, 1945

"It's the Calloway Boogie, keeps you groovy
24 hours a day."
From the jazz recording *The Calloway Boogie*, Cab Calloway & his Orchestra, 1947

See also the jazz recordings *Boy, It's Solid Groovy*, Jimmy Smith & his Sepians, 1941, and *Groovy Like A Movie – Let's Get Groovy*, Bonnie Davis & The Piccadilly Pipers, 1944 (The B-side of the latter was called *I Don't Stand For That Jive*.)

Ground smashers

Shoes or feet

Gumshoe

1. Detective, private eye

2. To creep around, to look for clues

Gunsel

Originally a term for a young person, punk, eventually it was used as a general word for a tough-guy or gunman
"Let's give them the gunsel. He actually did shoot Thusby and Jacobi, didn't he? Anyway, he's made to order for the part, look at him. Let's give him to them."
Humphrey Bogart giving Elisha Cook Jnr a hard time, from the film *The Maltese Falcon*, 1941

Gut-ripper   Knife, shiv
"Double-edged double-jointed springblade
cuts-all genuine Filipino twisty-handled all-
American gut-ripper."
From the short story collection *The Neon
Wilderness*, Nelson Algren, 1947

Gut scraper   Violinist

Guzzle shop   Bar, speakeasy

Hack	Automobile
Hack-jockey	Taxi driver
Half a yard	Fifty dollars
Half-hipped	Not very enlightened or sophisticated From the autobiography *Really The Blues*, Mezz Mezzrow and Bernard Wolfe, 1946
Half-stiffed	Tipsy, under the influence
Hand in your dinner pail	Die "He gives a big howl and hands in his dinner pail." From the novel *Dames Don't Care*, Peter Cheyney, 1937
Hand it to them	Shooting at someone
Hand out a line	Lie, bullshit
Hang out your hearing flap	Listen carefully
Hangin' it in	Having sex A phrase very popular with Jerry Lee Lewis.
Hanging paper	Passing forged cheques
Hanky panky	1. Sex 2. A whore "Helen wasn't no hanky-panky." From the novel *Red Harvest*, Dashiell Hammett, 1929
Hard boiled	Tough, streetwise "I like smooth shiny girls, hard-boiled and loaded with sin."

Philip Marlowe in the novel *Farewell My Lovely*, Raymond Chandler, 1940

"My God! For a fat, middle-aged, hard-boiled pig-headed guy, you've got the vaguest way of doing things I ever heard of ..."
Praise for the Continental Op, from the novel *Red Harvest*, Dashiell Hammett, 1929

A record by Lee Barth called *Onie Gagen* was described by a reviewer in August 1930 as "a comedy monologue in hard-boiled, tough-guy manner".

Harlem sunset	Bloodletting, knife wounds
Hash	Food
Hash house	Cheap eating establishment, where standards are not exactly top-of-the-range

"'If it's that kind of job, I hoped you picked a five dollar house. You're too young for the two-dollar trade, and personally I wouldn't like sailors.'
'I'm a waitress in a hash-house.'
'It rhymes up the same way.'"
From the novel *Mildred Pierce*, James M. Cain, 1943

"I'm sleeping in flophouses, eating in hash joints, mooching for dimes."
From the novel *Murder On Monday*, Robert Patrick Wilmot, 1952

Hash-slinger	A cook, especially in a fast food joint. See the jazz recording *Slingin' Hash*, Zoot Simms, 1950
Hatchet man	Assassin, strong-arm guy
Have one on the city	Drink some water

Have yourself a time	Go wild, push the boat out
Having your teeth pulled	Being disarmed "I pulled his teeth, boss. He was carrying a .32 in the shoulder holster." From the novel *A Hearse of Another Colour*, M.E.Chaber, 1959
Hay	1. Marijuana 2. Bed "I was nuts about her then. Who wouldn't be? All the boys were anxious to nudge her into the hay." From the novel *Death Is Confidential*, Lawrence Lariar, 1959
Hay parlour	Bedroom
He ain't worth the powder it'd take to blow his nose	I'm not impressed with him
He could stand one more greasing, he's not slick enough	He's not very impressive, a poor dresser or a poor performer
He got it with the rats and mice	He won it in a crap game See the novel *The Dain Curse*, Dashiell Hammett, 1928
He ought to have his wardrobe cleaned and burned	He dresses like a square
He'd put clothes on a fish	He's a smooth talker, a con artist, the kind that would sell you Christmas cards in June
He's just like the man in the casket – dead in there	He's cool, he's a hepcat

He's so sharp he's bleeding	That is one well dressed dude From the autobiography *I, Paid My Dues,* Babs Gonzales, 1967
Head in a sling	Troubled, weighed down with worry
Head knock	The boss, the person in charge
Headache stick	Police baton
Headlights	Breasts
Headshrinker	Psychiatrist Policeman: "Do you know if the boy ever talked to a psychiatrist?" Sal Mineo: "You mean a headshrinker?" From the film *Rebel Without A Cause,* 1955
Heap	Automobile eg: "So I hopped in the heap and tooled it downtown."
A heap of jack	Lots of money
Heaped to the gills	High on drugs
Heat	1. The law "Somebody called the heat They threw us all in jail. We had a lot of rhythm Nobody had their bail. The judge gave us a hearing, When he heard us play, He shouted for an encore In a real gone way, He hollered 'Wail, man, wail!'" From the rockabilly recording *Wail, Man, Wail,* Kip Tyler & The Flips, 1957 2. Weapons
Heat-making gown	Low-cut dress
Heater	Gun

"All right dad, shed the heater ..."
From the short story *Goldfish*, Raymond
Chandler, *Black Mask* magazine, June
1936

Heavy sugar   A large amount of money

Heebie-jeebies   Fear, apprehension, the shakes
                           "Keep it up and you're going to have the
                           heebie-jeebies for fair, a nervous break-
                           down."
                           From the novel *Red Harvest*,
                           Dashiell Hammett, 1929

                           See the jazz recording *Heebie Jeebies*,
                           Louis Armstrong's Hot Five, Feb 1926

                           Ethel Waters released a blues called
                           Heebie Jeebies in 1926, for which the
                           Columbia Records adverts read: "You all
                           know the 'heebie jeebies'. Perhaps you've
                           had them before. You just can't keep
                           still ..."

                           When B.B.King was still a DJ in the early
                           1950s, he ran a radio show in Memphis
                           called *Heebie Jeebies*.

Heel   A louse, a punk, a bum
                           "Which one of you heels scratched the
                           guy at West Cimmaron last night?"
                           From the short story *Finger Man*,
                           Raymond Chandler, *Black Mask*
                           magazine, October 1934

Heel-beater   Dancer

Heel the joint   Leave without paying

Heeled   Packing a gun

Heist   A robbery or theft

Hell bent   Determined

Hen pen   Female prison

Hep

1. Hip, cool, righteous, in the know
"They said they were going to a real hep party, and that kind of party I'm still scared of, mister. I don't go to them."
ie: A drug party.
From the novel *Violent Night*, Whit Harrison, 1952

"'You're a thriller,' she told him. 'Where'd you get so hep?'"
From the novel *Go, Man Go!*, Edward De Roo, 1959

Mitchell's Jazz Kings released a song called *Hep* in 1922, Cab Calloway & his Orchestra made a jazz record called *(Hep Hep) The Jumping Jive* in 1939, and even Fred Astaire put out a record in 1940 called *Dig It (I Ain't Hep To That Step, But I'll Dig It)* ie: I haven't seen that dance before, but I'll soon get the hang of it.

2. To inform someone, to put them wise
The word was being used in this sense by street gangs in the early years of the 20th century, as reported in the book *Apaches Of New York*, A.H. Lewis, 1912

See the jazz recording *We The Cats Shall Hep Ya*, Cab Calloway & his Orchestra, 1944

Hepcat

One who is hep, totally uncubistic
Down Beat's 1939 Yearbook of Swing defined a hepcat as "1. A swing devotee who is 'hep' or alert to the most authoritative information, or 2. A swing musician."

Lavada Durst, a 1950s DJ with station KVET, Austin, Texas, broadcast under the name of Dr. Hepcat. He published a slang booklet in 1953 entitled *The Jives of Dr. Hepcat*.

Lawrence Lariar describes a nightclub on Fifty Second Street in New York in his 1959 novel *Death Is Confidential*: "Hardly enough room to swing a hep-cat in. The last time I counted the tables, there were just two dozen. The take can't be much for Ziggi, unless he's selling reefers on the side."

See the jazz recording *Hep Cat Love Song*, Cab Calloway & his Orchestra, 1941

Here's how   A toast when drinking

Here's your hat,   Get lost, go away
what's your hurry?

Hey-hey   1. Sex

        2. A disturbance, a fuss

Hi-pockets   Nickname for a tall guy (The corresponding nickname for someone short is Pee Wee.)
In 1953, country music DJ Hi-Pockets Duncan from KDAV, Lubbock, Texas, gave Buddy Holly his first radio exposure, and briefly became the singer's first manager.

Hick   Country bumpkin, unsophisticated
"Whadda you hicks do around here for kicks?"
From the film *The Wild One*, 1954

Hide   A set of drums

High and fly and   Something, or someone, very good,
too wet to dry   pleasing

High-hat   Stuck up, putting on airs
"Look here gal don't you high-hat me
I ain't forgot what you used to be
When you didn't have nothin'

That was plain to see,
Don't get above your raisin'
Stay down to earth with me."
From the bluegrass recording
Don't Get Above Your Raisin',
Lester Flatt, Earl Scruggs & The Foggy
Mountain Boys, 1951

High roller   Ostentatious or heavy gambler

High tone   Fashionable, expensive

High sign   Signal, significant gesture, ok, warning
"One of his yegg men sat by the doors
has seen me and has given his boss the
high sign."
From the novel *Killers Don't Care*,
Rod Callahan, 1950

High-tail it   Run away, leave in a hurry

High, wide and handsome   Doing well, everything A-ok
"Jake married her after he left here and
moved to New York – after he was riding
high, wide and handsome. It must be
quite a comedown for her, living like she
has to now."
From the novel *Savage Night*, Jim
Thompson, 1953

See the country recording
High, Wide and Handsome,
Tex Ritter, 1935

Himalayas   Chest
"Baby, you got the Himalayas knocked
into a sombrero."
From the novel *Grin And Dare It*, Ricky
Drayton, 1953, which continues in the
following vein: "She had the kind of
curves to make 3D seem flat; however
drunk she got she could never have fallen
flat on her face; she couldn't have stood
against a wall without opening a
window."

89

Hincty	Paranoid, nervous
Hip	In the know, worldly wise, clever, enlightened, sophisticated See the jazz recordings *Hip! Hip!,* Jack Stillman's Orioles, 1925; *Hip Chic,* Duke Ellington & his Famous Orchestra, 1938; *Stop Pretending (So Hip You See),* Buddy Johnson & his Band, 1939; and the blues recording *You Done Got Hip,* Roosevelt Sykes, 1942
Hip to the tip	The pinnacle of hipness, a righteous dude
Hip your ship	To inform, to tell you something
Hipped	To understand, to possess knowledge, to be convinced of something "You're still hipped on Medley as a killer? Hell, Frank, it doesn't make sense." From the novel *The Lenient Beast,* Fredric Brown, 1957
Hipster	"Someone who's in the know, grasps everything, is alert." From the autobiography *Really The Blues,* Mezz Mezzrow and Bernard Wolfe, 1946 "One who is well schooled in the hep world." From the booklet *The Jives Of Doctor Hepcat,* Lavada Durst, 1953
Hit	Underworld contract killing
Hit man	Assassin
Hit the bottle high	Get drunk "Before you start hittin' that bottle over there, I want to do you a small favour, if you'll let me." From the novel *The Man With The Golden Arm,* Nelson Algren, 1949

See the jazz recording *Hittin' The Bottle*, Frankie Trumbauer, 1930

Hit the bricks
1. Leave

2. Walk the streets

Hit the hay
1. Go to sleep
"Alright, precious, you'd better hit the hay. You sound all-in."
From the film *The Maltese Falcon*, 1941

2. Smoke marijuana

Hit the skids
To be down on your luck, busted and generally behind the eight ball

Hit the wall
To break out of prison

Hitched up
One night stand
"I went out last night,
'an I got hitched up ..."
From the rockabilly recording *She Said*, Hasil Adkins, 1964

Hittin' the hop
On drugs

Hittin' the jug
Serious drinking
"Well out to the dance hall
And cut a little rug,
Oh we're runnin' like wildfire,
An' a hittin' that jug ..."
From the rockabilly recording *We Wanna Boogie*, Sonny Burgess & The Pacers, 1956

Hobo jungle
Tramp settlement or camp

Hoister
Pickpocket

Hold onto your chair and don't step on no snakes
Listen up, get ready, brace yourself

Hole in the wall
Low class joint, cheap bar
"No windows, no doors,

just a hole in the wall ..."
From the boogie recording *Chicken Shack Boogie*, Amos Milburn, 1946

Holed up

In hiding

Holding

In possession of drugs

Holding down a package

Intoxicated, plastered, several drinks past the point of no return
"I was holding down a lovely package."comments Dashiell Hammett's Continental Op in a story from the 1920s called *The Golden Horseshoe*

Holding on

"Just remember the words of the great Joe E. Lewis. He said 'You're not drunk if you can lay on the floor without holdin' on.'"
Dean Martin onstage at The Sands, Las Vegas, February 1964

Holler

Yell
"I wiggled and I hollered,
Screamed and I cried,
Don't shoot me baby,
I'm too young to die ..."
From the rockabilly recording *Don't Shoot Me Baby*, Bill Bowen & The Rockets, 1956

Honey

Good looking woman, a real doll

Honky tonk

Bar, juke joint, spit and sawdust club
"The honk-a-tonk last night was well attended by ball-heads, bachelors and leading citizens."
From *The Daily Ardmorite,* Ardmore, Oklahoma, February 24th 1891, quoted by Nick Tosches in the *Blackwell Guide To Recorded Country Music.*

"I'm a honky tonk man,
and I can't seem to stop.
I love to give the girls a whirl

to the music of that old jukebox . . ."
From the rockabilly recording *Honky
Tonk Man,* Johnny Horton, 1956

The Emerson Military Band released
the *Honky Tonk Rag* in 1917, and
Bennie Moten's Kansas City Orchestra
put out a jazz record in 1925 called
Sister Honky Honk.

See also the country recordings *Honky
Tonk Blues,* Al Dexter, 1936 and *I'm
Going To Get Me A Honky Tonky Baby,*
Buddy Jones, 1941

Sophie Tucker starred in a film called
Honky Tonk for Warner Brothers in
1929.

Honky tonk angel   Good-time girl
"Let them honkytonkin' angels
be the girls I'll never love,
let 'em know it's you I'm cravin',
it's you I'm thinkin' of . . ."
From the country recording
Let the Jukebox Keep on Playing,
Carl Perkins, 1955

Honky tonk hotel   A low class flophouse
"It's funny, anyway. That girl had class,
yet she was living in that honky tonk
hotel."
From the novel *The Lady In The
Morgue,* Jonathan Latimer, 1936

Hooch   Alcohol
"Keep away from bootleg hooch
When you're on a spree,
Take good care of yourself
You belong to me."
From the jazz recording *Button Up Your
Overcoat,* Ruth Etting, 1929

Hooch hound   Drunkard

Hoochie-coocher

Striptease artist
"Folks now here's the story
bout Minnie The Moocher
she was a red-hot
hoochie-coocher."
From the jazz recording *Minnie The Moocher*, Cab Calloway & his Orchestra, 1931

See also the blues recording *Hoochy Coochy Blues*, Lemuel Fowler, 1926

Hood

Hoodlum, mobster, tough-guy
"The crime climate had changed greatly since the wild and lunatic Twenties. The big hoods were now businessmen and owned hotels and summer resorts and distilleries."
From the novel *Little Men, Big World*, W.R. Burnett, 1951

See the jazz recording *March of the Hoodlums*, Eddie Lang, 1930

Hooey

Lies, rubbish

Hoof

1. Feet

2. Dance

Hoofery

Dancehall

Hoofing it

1. Walking

2. Dancing

Hooks

Hands, fingers

Hoosegow

Prison
"Trundle him off to the hoosegow – he'd look nice in a pair of bracelets."
Waldo Lydecker in the film *Laura*, 1944

Hop

1. Drugs

94

2. A dance party
"You know I got my hot-rod down the shop
Gotta meet my baby at the Teen Town hop."
From the R&B jump recording *Teen Town Hop*, The Philharmonics, 1958

See the jazz recording *Wednesday Night Hop*, Andy Kirk & his Twelve Clouds Of Joy, 1937, the same outfit who cut a tune called *What's Your Story, Morning Glory?* in 1938
See also the vocal group recording *At The Hop*, Danny & The Juniors, 1957

Hop in my kemp and take off for the cashbah

"Get in my car and go to Lovers' Lane"
From the film *High School Confidential*, 1958

Hop joint

Place where drugs are bought or smoked
"Went in the hop joint
smoking the pills,
in walked a sheriff from Jericho
Hill . . ."
From the hillbilly boogie recording *Cocaine Blues*, Roy Hogshed, 1948

Hophead

Drug addict
See the jazz recording *Hop Head*, Duke Ellington & The Washingtonians, 1927

Hopped up

1. Intoxicated, drugged up
"You're a friend of mine, remember? You got the brass down on you. A hopped-up hood tried to kill you."
From the novel *Violent Night*, Whit Harrison, 1952

2. Customised car
"Say, this baby really rolls along,
is she hopped up?"

95

From the film *The Devil Thumbs A Ride*, 1947

Hopping a freight
Hitching a ride on a freight train
"'During the depression,' said the cowboy to me, 'I used to hop freights at least once a month. In those days you'd see hundreds of men riding a flatcar . . .'"
From the novel *On The Road*, Jack Kerouac, 1957

Horn
1. Trumpet

2. Telephone

Horse feathers
Rubbish, bullshit
See the jazz recording *Horse Feathers*, Cliff Jackson & his Krazy Kats, 1930

"'We pretended to be struggling for the gun. I fell over the carpet.'
'Ah, horse feathers!'"
Joel Cairo fails to convince the police, From the film *The Maltese Falcon*, 1941

Hosed down
Riddled with bullets

Hot car
1. Fast car

2. Stolen car, one the police are looking for
"My Cad would be hotter than a strip-teaser's tassel by now . . ."
Shell Scott realizes that the cops have a description of his car, from the novel *Always Leave 'Em Dying*, Richard S. Prather, 1961

Hot circle
A great record, a wild waxing, one of the platters that matter

Hot little mouse
Good looking woman, a real gone chick
"He told me he was running around with

a hot little mouse named Leona Sandmark."
From the novel *Halo In Blood*, Howard Browne, 1946

Hot in the zipper   Sexually aroused, amorous

The hot lead treatment   Getting shot

Hot man   A good jazz musician, capable of playing the hippest music
There was a jazz band in the Storyville district of New Orleans in 1910 called The Four Hot Hounds, and Joe 'King' Oliver was one of the members.

Hot pillow joint   Cheap motel renting rooms by the hour

Hot-seat fodder   Criminal

Hot squat   The electric chair
Erle Stanley Gardner wrote a story called *The Hot Squat* for the October 1931 issue of *Black Mask* magazine.

Hotcha   Expression of enjoyment in hipster circles, popular in the Twenties and Thirties
There was a venue in Harlem in 1932 called Club Hotcha.

Hotcha number   A good looking woman

Hotrod   Fast or customised car
"O'Brian got out of the car. He said 'You ought to drive hot rods, Ed.'
'I would. Except for my mother. She's queen of the dirt tracks. She'd be jealous if I muscled in.'"
From the novel *Violent Night*, Whit Harrison, 1952

"Dig that crazy driver,
yeah dig that fool a hole.
Dig it down by the side of the road,
he can hear them hotrods roll ..."

From the rockaiblly recording *Dig That Crazy Driver*, William Pennix, 1956

Hotsy-totsy

Fine and dandy, really good
The word hotsy was originally a slang term for a prostitute.

Prolific jazz bandleader Irving Mills ran an outfit in the late Twenties called Irving Mills & his Hotsy Totsy Gang.

See the jazz recording *Everything Is Hotsy Totsy Now*, The California Ramblers, 1925

Hotter than a two-dollar pistol

Sought-after, in demand, whether for reasons of popularity or because you're wanted by the police
"I was dead broke, on the lam, and as hot as a two-dollar pistol with the authorities everywhere."
From the autobiography *Rap Sheet*, Blackie Audett, 1955

Hotwire

To start a car without the use of keys

House hop

Rent party, a dance in someone's apartment

House peeper

Hotel detective

How come you do me like you do?

Why do you treat me this way?
See the jazz recording *How Come You Do Me Like You Do?*, Rudy Vallee, 1930

How do you like them apples?

How does that grab you?
What do you think of that?

How's the grouch bag holding?

Do you have any money on you?

Hum Dum Dinger From Dingersville

Beautiful girl, a total knockout
See the country recordings
She's A Hum Dum Dinger,
Buddy Jones, 1941, and *She's A Hum*

Ding Mama, Jack Hilliard & Leslie
Palmer, 1938

Hung up 1. Worried, anxious

2. Fascinated

Hungry "I'm so hungry I could eat the raw right
stump of General Sherman."
From the novel *Kiss Tomorrow Goodbye*,
Horace McCoy, 1949

Hunky dory Ok, in order, fine
"There was I talking to myself,
Feeling hunky dory,
A pretty girl passed by,
I tried to catch her eye,
She seemed to sigh
'Hey, what's his story?'"
From the jazz recording *What's his
Story*, Harry "The Hipster" Gibson, 1946

The Columbia Orchestra released a
record called *Hunky Dory* in 1901.

Hush house Speakeasy, illegal gin-joint

Hush-hush Secret

Hymn-hustler Priest, sky pilot, bible-basher

I ain't comin' on that tab	I don't agree with you
I ain't saying you're wrong, but I ain't saying you're right either	Diplomacy, the Jim Thompson way, from the novel *Pop. 1280*, 1964
I am cable and able to wake you	I'm about to let you know what's happening
I dig your lick	I understand what you're saying
I don't know beans	I haven't a clue, your guess is as good as mine
I don't mean maybe, baby	That's right, I really mean it, that's what I want to do
I don't go for that magoo	Don't hand me that line, I'm not falling for that kind of talk
I don't sound you	I don't understand you
I feel like Death Valley	I'm thirsty
I get it, but I don't want it	I hear what you're saying, but I don't like it
I got a lot of room in my ears yet	Keep talking, I'm listening
I got your signal clear and cool	I understand you perfectly From the film *High School Confidential*, 1958
I have heard the wind blow before	You're bluffing, don't hand me that line

100

I tried to carry a stuffed moose head through a revolving door	Somebody beat me up From the novel *The Bedroom Bolero*, Michael Avallone, 1963
I wanna jump your bones	I'd like to sleep with you
Ice	1. Jewels 2. To kill someone
Iceberg act	Playing it cool
Iceman	Professional killer
Ickie	"One who does not understand swing music." From *Down Beat's Yearbook of Swing*, *1939* "One of the upper crust, big shot, bankers, money people." From the booklet *The Jives Of Doctor Hepcat*, Lavada Durst, 1953
I'd rather drink muddy water, and sleep in a hollow log	I'm not interested "Rather drink muddy water, sleep in a hollow log, than to be in Atlanta treated like a dirty dog." From the country recording *T For Texas (Blue Yodel No. 1)*, Jimmie Rodgers, 1927
If I'm lyin' I'm flyin'	I'm telling the truth, I swear
If she don't bake, she doesn't get dusted	If she doesn't pay, she doesn't get any narcotics From the film *High School Confidential*, 1958
If that don't turn you on, brother, you ain't got no switches	That should impress you – if not, then you're probably dead already

If that's good then my feet are kippers	I'm not impressed
I'm fresh out of a chatterbox	I don't have a machine gun
I'm gonna tear your playhouse down	You're in trouble, I'm going to make you pay, you'll be sorry "I caught you out, runnin' round, now I'm a-gonna tear your playhouse down." From the rockabilly recording *Nothin' But A Nuthin*, Jimmy Stewart & his Nighthawks, 1957 See the blues recording *I'm Gonna Tear Your Playhouse Down*, Hazel Myers, 1924
In a bluesey groove	Depressed, low down
In a heap	Completely drunk
In a pig's eye	That's rubbish, I don't agree with you
In dutch	In trouble with someone, in their bad books "We ain't never been in dutch We don't browse around too much Don't bother us, leave us alone Anyway, we almost grown." From the rock'n'roll recording *Almost Grown*, Chuck Berry, 1959
In like Flynn	A certainty, a sure thing, deriving from popular stories of Errol Flynn's success with women
In my book you're way upstairs	I really like you, I'm impressed
In the bag	Drunk "He had been drinking steadily since his return from the Arizona Club nearly twenty four hours earlier and yet one

who did not know him well could never have told from his speech, his walk, or his visible reflexes that he was in the bag."
From the novel of the screenplay of *Ocean's Eleven*, George Clayton Johnson and Jack Golden Russell, 1960

In the grip of the grape   Drunk

In the groove   Just right, solid, A-ok, righteous
Defined in *Down Beat's 1939 Year Book of Swing* as "1. Playing genuine swing, and 2. Carried away by the music"

"She's in the groove, right on the ball she's reet, petite and gone ..."
From the R&B jump jive recording *Reet, Petite and Gone*,
Louis Jordan & The Tympany Five, 1947

In there   Groovy, fine as wine, hip
"Now I'd say this chick is really in there ..."
From the jazz recording *The Hipster's Blues, Opus 7½*,
Harry "The Hipster" Gibson, 1944

Indoor aviator   Elevator attendant

Interviewing your brains   Thinking

Iron   1. Kill
eg: "To iron someone out."

2. Gun
"'I'm keeping your gun,' Rudy went on. 'I'm taking any iron that Carol has when she shows.'"
From the novel *The Getaway*, Jim Thompson, 1958

Iron bungalow   Prison

Iron men

Dollars
"'Hundred dollars,' I said. 'Iron men, fish, bucks to the number of one hundred ...'"
From the novel *Farewell My Lovely*, Raymond Chandler, 1940

It

1. Sex appeal
Clara Bow, one of the most famous movie stars of the 1920s, had a huge success with a film called *It*. The sign on her grave at Forest Lawn cemetery reads "Hollywood's 'It' Girl".

See the jazz recording *I've Got 'It', But it Don't Do Me No Good*, Helen Kane, 1930

2. Sex organs
"You gotta wet it,
you gotta wet it,
dampen it so it can grow,
you gotta wet it,
you gotta wet it,
dampen it farmer you know,
sprinkle it and dampen it
and let the good work go on."
From the boogie-woogie recording *Wet It*, Frankie "Half-Pint" Jaxon, 1937

"You didn't want it when you had it
so I got another man,
keep your hands off it,
it don't belong to you."
From the blues recording *Take Your Hand Off It*, Lil Johnson, 1937

See also the blues recordings *She Done Sold It Out*, The Memphis Jug Band, 1934; *Try And Get It!*, Bea Foote, 1938; *I Want Every Bit Of It*, Bessie Smith, 1926

3. Virginity
See the jazz recording *She Really Meant To Keep It*, Johnny Messner & his Orchestra, c.1940

104

It fits in with the beat	That suits the occasion, that's appropriate
It fries my wig	It blows my mind, I'm impressed, I'm astonished
It looks like rain	Someone is about to get arrested
It turns my crank	I like it, I approve, it turns me on
It will pull you dead to the curb	It'll knock you out, you'll love it
It wound up in smoke	It ended in gunfire
It's a natural gas that you can't zig a zag	You can't mend something that's broken, you can't fight City Hall, it's a hopeless case
It's all right, I make it fresh every morning	I'm paying the bill, don't worry, I've got plenty of money From the film *Johnny O'Clock*, 1947
It's git down time	This is it, something's about to happen Git down time is traditionally the time of the evening when prostitutes start work.
I've got to take a rub-down in water	I need a bath
Ivories	1.Piano keys "Here's a cat that lays a group of ivory talking trash and strictly putting down a gang of jive." ie: He's a really good piano player. From the booklet *The Jives Of Doctor Hepcat*, Lavada Durst, 1953 James P. Johnson, the blues, stride and boogie pianist was billed as "King of the Ivories" when appearing at the New Star Casino in New York in February 1922.

2. Teeth

Ixnay   No (backslang for nix)

Izzatso?   Really, you don't say? (Is that so?)

J.D.

Juvenile delinquent
"The rock'n'rollers, the Twisters, the hipsters, the teenage J.D.s, all inside with their black leather, black denim, black hair, black eyes and black hearts."
From the novel *Twilight Girls*, Judson Grey, 1962

Jack

1. Money
"The place is lousy with jack ..."
ie: There's lots of money at that nightclub we're going to rob.
From the novel *Little Caesar*, W.R. Burnett, 1929

"All the jack he'd made in the rackets was gone. The state had latched on to part of it and the federal government had taken another big bite and lawyers had eaten up the rest."
From the novel *Savage Night*, Jim Thompson, 1953

2. All-purpose term of address between hipsters, sometimes lengthened to Jackson

Jack rabbit blood

Habitual prison escaper, said to have jack rabbit blood because of their continual tendency to run away

Jacket

1. A prisoner's file, both positive and negative, kept throughout the duration of their sentence

2. The sentence for a particular crime
"He'd been in short pants in the days when Louie Fomorowski was beating two murder raps. They'd gotten a one-to-life jacket on him for the second one, of which he'd served nine months in privileged circumstances."

From the novel *The Man With The Golden Arm*, Nelson Algren, 1949

Jackroller

Pickpocket, mugger, purse-snatcher

Jailbait

1. Underage girl
See the novel *Jailbait*, William Bernard, 1951

2. Someone destined for prison
"'Are you interested in that?'
'What's it to you?'
'That's jail bait.'
'He's just a kid.'
'Yeah, that's what I said once. Maybe you'll be lucky. Maybe they won't send him back to prison. Maybe he'll get himself killed first.'"
From the film *They Live By Night*, 1948

Jalopy

Automobile, not usually of the newest variety
"We got a ride from a couple of fellows – wranglers, teenagers, country boys in a put-together jalopy."
From the novel *On The Road*, Jack Kerouac, 1957

Jake

1. Correct, alright, in order, ok
"'Stick-up,' he said. 'Be very quiet and everything will be jake.'"
From the novel *Farewell, My Lovely*, Raymond Chandler, 1940

2. All purpose term of address between hipsters
See the R&B jump jive recording *Jake, What A Shake*, Louis Jordan & The Tympany Five, 1939

3. Moonshine liquor

Jam-up

Something really good

Jane

Woman, girl

"You said he or she – do you think
maybe it was a jane did the croaking?"
From the novel *The Corrupt Ones*,
J.C. Barton, c. 1950

"I can't let you in just now. Ya *see*,
I got a jane inside . . ."
From the film *The Public Enemy*, 1933

Jass
Jazz music, written both ways from 1913
up until around 1920, when the word
Jazz became the accepted spelling
In New Orleans in the 1890s there was a
snappily-titled proto-jazz outfit called The
Razzy Dazzy Spasm Band. Nick La
Rocca's Original Dixieland Jazz Band
were formed in 1915, and they put out
the *Dixie Jass Band One-Step* in January
1917. In November 1917 they released
At The Jass Band Ball, while by March
1918 it had become *At The Jazz Band
Ball*. W.C. Handy put out a record called
That Jazz Dance in 1917, credited to
Handy's Orchestra of Memphis, while in
June 1917 The Frisco Jazz Band put out
a song called the *Johnson 'Jass' Blues*.

Java
Coffee
"Gimme a shot of java, nix on the
moo-juice." ie: A cup of coffee, no
milk.
From the autobiography *Really The
Blues*, Mezz Mezzrow and Bernard Wolfe,
1946

See the vocal group recording *Java Jive*,
The Ink Spots, 1946

Jazz
Having sex, or sexual fluids
"'Jesus!' she jeered. 'The nicest looking
guy I ever saw and you turn out to be a
lousy snooping copper. How much? I
don't jazz cops.'"
From the novel *The Killer Inside Me*,
Jim Thompson, 1952

See *The Jazz Me Blues*, Lucille
Hegamin, 1920; *I Want A Jazzy Kiss*,
Mamie Smith, 1921; *I Wanna Jazz
Some More,* Kitty Brown, 1924

Jazz baby

Jazz fan, usually a girl or flapper of the
1920s
See the jazz recordings *Jazz Baby*, Jim
Europe's 369th Infantry 'Hell Fighters'
Band, March 1919, and the *Jazz Babies
Ball*, Maceo Pinkard, 1920

Jazz water

Bootleg alcohol
John Joseph wrote a story called *Jazz
Water – By Special Delivery* for the May
1924 issue of *Black Mask* magazine,
which advertised it as "The romance of
the hooch".

Jazzbo

Boyfriend

Jelly roll

Sex organs
"Jelly roll, jelly roll,
Laying on the fence,
If you don't try to get it
You ain't got no sense ..."
From *You've Got To Save That Thing*,
Ora Alexander, 1931

See the blues recordings
*I Ain't Gonna Give Nobody None Of
This Jelly Roll*, Dabney's Novelty
Orchestra, 1919; *Nobody In Town Can
Bake A Jelly Roll Like Mine*, Bessie
Smith, 1923; *Jelly Whippin' Blues*,
Tampa Red, 1928; *You'll Never Miss
Your Jelly Till Your Jelly Roller's Gone*,
Lil Johnson, 1929; and the disarmingly
modest *I Got The Best Jelly Roll In
Town*, Lonnie Johnson, 1930

Jerks & fillies

Boys and girls, cats and kittens, studs and
sisters
"Jerks and Fillies" was DJ Gene Noble's

all-pupose name for callers to his show on WLAC Nashville in the 1950s.

Jim

All purpose hipster term of address, usually uncomplimentary

Jitterbug

1. Jazz dance

2. Someone who dances to jazz
Defined rather snottily by *Down Beat's Yearbook Of Swing*, 1939, as "A swing fan (not a true swing music lover) who expresses his fondness for swing music by eccentric dancing or emotional gestures and gyrations."

See the jazz recordings *Lullaby To A Jitterbug*, The Andrews Sisters, 1938, and *Jitterbugs Broke It Down*, Ollie Shepard, 1940

Jive

1. "v. To kid, to talk insincerely or without meaning, to use an elaborate or misleading line. n. Confusing doubletalk, pretentious conversation, anything false or phony."
From the autobiography *Really The Blues*, Mezz Mezzrow and Bernard Wolfe, 1946

Down Beat's Yearbook Of Swing 1939 defined the word merely as "the language of swing", however, they also list "Jive artist" as "an elegant nothing, a ham who sells out".

Cab Calloway publicised his own booklets of jive slang with the recording *Jive (Page One Of The Hepster's Dictionary),* Cab Calloway & his Orchestra, 1938, and *Jiveformation Please*, Cab Calloway & his Orchestra, 1938

The word shows up in numerous jazz and blues recordings, for instance: *Don't Jive*

111

Me, Louis Armstrong's Hot Five, 1928;
State Street Jive, Cow Cow Davenport
& Ivy Smith, 1928; *Sweet Jivin' Mama*,
Blind Blake, 1929; *Jive Man Blues*,
Frankie 'Half-Pint' Jaxon, 1929; and the
succinctly-titled *Jive*, Duke Ellington & his
Famous Orchestra, 1932

See also *Jive Bomber*, recorded in
London during the Blitz by Stephane
Grappelly & his Quartet. Another jazz-
related response to the Luftwaffe came in
1941 from Una Mae Carlisle with a song
called *Blitzkrieg Baby (You Can't Bomb
Me)*.

Many rock'n'roll DJs of the fifties used
the name Doctor Jive, the most famous
being Tommy Smalls of WWRL, New
York City.

2. Marijuana
See the jazz recording *Here Comes The
Man With The Jive*, Stuff Smith & his
Onyx Club Boys, 1936

3. Insulting term of address, short for jive-
ass motherfucker

Jive stick	A marijuana cigarette
Jive that makes it drip	Clouds that produce rain From the autobiography *Really The Blues*, Mezz Mezzrow and Bernard Wolfe, 1946
Joe below	"A musician who pays less than union scale." From *Down Beat's Yearbook of Swing*, 1939
John Hancock	Signature
Johnny-on-the-spot	Right place, right time eg: "Say the word and I'll be Johnny-on-

the-spot." ie: I'm there when you need
me.
"Friend you go out in a hall
Want the joint to rock,
All you do is give us a call
We'll be johnny on the spot."
From the rock'n'roll recording
Rockin' Is Our Bizness, The Treniers,
1956

Joint   Place, venue, establishment

Jolt   1. A shot of alcohol
                     "Sighing heavily I walked to the liquor
                     cabinet and refilled my glass – this time
                     with straight booze. I needed a good jolt
                     and I planned on getting it."
                     From the novel *Two Timing Tart*,
                     John Davidson, 1961

                     2. A shot of dope
                     "Once they get used to the jolts, they
                     need four or five of them in a day. That'll
                     cost anywhere from five dollars to ten
                     dollars. I've found kids who spent their
                     lunch money for dope."
                     From the novel *The Deadly Lover*,
                     Robert O. Saber, 1951

Joy ride   Having sex

Judas hole   Small hole in the door of a speakeasy

Juice   Alcohol
                     See the jazz recording *Buy Me Some
                     Juice*, Blue Lu Barker, with Danny
                     Barker's Fly Cats, 1939

Juiced   Drunk
                     "Let's drink some juice
                     Let's all get loose . . ."
                     From the R&B recording *Juiced,*
                     Jackie Brenston & his Delta Cats, 1952

Juke joint   Cheap bar with dancing facilities

"Your nerves are jumping like a
juke joint on saturday night."
From the novel *Halo In Blood*,
Howard Browne, 1946

"Well there's a little juke joint
On the outskirts of town,
Where the cats pick 'em up
And they lay them down . . ."
From the rock'n'roll recording
Dance To The Bop,
Gene Vincent & The Blue Caps,
1957

Jump street   The beginning of something

Jumping   Wild, uninhibited
"Check your weapons at the door,
Be sure to pay your quarter,
Burn your leather on the floor,
Grab anybody's daughter.
The roof is rockin',
The neighbours are knockin',
We're all bums when the wagon comes
I mean this joint is jumpin.'"
From the jazz recording *The Joint Is
Jumpin'*, Fats Waller & his Rhythm,
1937

Jumped up   Arrested, cornered by the police

Jungled up   Living arrangements
eg: "He's jungled up over in the Bronx"
ie: He's got a room somewhere in
the Bronx.

Just for kicks   For a laugh, for the hell of it

Keep plant

Keep watch, act as lookout, stay in one place

Keep your lamps on the prowl

Keep a lookout, keep your eyes peeled

Keep your nickel out of it

Keep your opinions to yourself, stay out of this
"Keep your nickel out of this, wise guy."
From the novel *Red Gardenias*, Jonathan Latimer, 1939

Kick

"The kind of music you like, dance, cigarette or movie."
From the booklet *The Jives Of Doctor Hepcat*, Lavada Durst, 1953

Kick off

To die, expire, bite the dust
"'Another one kicked off on us, Captain.'
'How many times do I have to tell you that a man can die in jail just the same as in hospital?'"
From the novel *A Walk On The Wild Side,* Nelson Algren, 1957

Kicking the gong around

Smoking opium
See the jazz recording *Kicking The Gong Around*, Cab Calloway & his Orchestra, 1931

Kicks

Thrills, excitement, a good time
"'I don't like you when you're with them.'
'Ah, it's all right, it's just kicks. We only live once. We're having a good time.'"
From the novel *On The Road*, Jack Kerouac, 1957

Meanwhile, back in the world of drugs, the soon-to-expire Mr. Birk is explaining his philosophy:
"'And you take it for kicks?'
'Kicks. Experience. Knowledge. Or some-

times, just plain old euphoria. You do dig
euphoria, don't you?' he leered."
From the novel *The Icepick In Ollie
Birk*, Eunice Sudak, 1966

Kicksville

Something enjoyable, a blast, the state of
getting your kicks
"A voiceless roar issued from a half-dozen
throats. The excitement of it, the thrill of
it, spread through the group like wildfire.
This was Kicksville! This was the utmost!"
From the novel *Run Tough, Run Hard*,
Carson Bingham, 1961

Killer diller

A knockout, the best, something truly hep
"Every band has a favourite killer-diller,
which is sure to be included on almost
every program they broadcast."
From Professor Cab Calloway's
Swingformation Bureau, early 1940s

"'They call him Zand. He's a killer.'
Joe and the other boys laughed. Reisman
eyed them steadily. 'How do you mean?'
'Sharpest dresser in town. Poiple shoits!
He'll moidah ya – ya bum!'"
From the novel *Little Men, Big World*,
W.R. Burnett, 1951

See the jazz recordings *Killer Diller*,
Benny Goodman & his Orchestra, 1937,
and *Killer Diller*, Gene Coy & his Killer
Dillers,1948

King bee

A stud, a ladykiller, top of the heap
"I'm a king bee baby,
buzzin' round your hive.
I can make honey,
let me come inside ..."
From the rockabilly recording
Got Love If You Want It,
Warren Smith, 1957

King Kong

Moonshine, bootleg whiskey
"On the second floor was a King Kong

116

speakeasy, where you could get yourself five-cent and ten-cent shots of home-brewed corn."
From the autobiography *Really The Blues*, Mezz Mezzrow and Bernard Wolfe, 1946

Kisser
Mouth or lips
"Chuck had the kisser of a clown, the wide-open, honest, boyish smile of the natural buffoon."
From the novel *Death Is Confidential*, Lawrence Lariar, 1959

Kitten
Girl
"Where are you carrying the heater, kitten?"
From the novel *Kiss Me, Deadly*, Mickey Spillane, 1953

Kitty
All-purpose term of address between hipsters

Knee pad
To beg

Knock a scarf
To eat

Knock a statue act
Hold on, wait a minute

Knock fowl soup
To die

Knock me a kiss
Kiss me

Knock over
Rob

Knock the polish off your toes
To dance
"Well my old gal's slow and easy,
All the hepcats know.
She gets that boppin' beat
She knocks the polish off her toes."
From *Put Your Cat Clothes On*, Carl Perkins, 1957

Knocked out
Drunk, intoxicated

Knockin' a jug	Getting drunk See the blues recording *Let's Knock A Jug*, Frankie 'Half-Pint' Jaxon, 1929
Know where the beat is	"To understand Swing." From *Down Beat's Yearbook of Swing, 1939*
Know your groceries	To be hip, aware, alert to the situation, to do things well, be accomplished Peter Cheyney has a variant on this in his 1943 novel *You Can Always Duck*: "The guy who threw this Chez Clarence dump together knew his vegetables."
Knowledge box	Head, brain
Knowledge box hitting on all cylinders	Intelligent, a smart customer

L7

A square, totally cubistic
A shape that can be made using both
thumbs and both forefingers.

Lacquer crackers

Records, platters, waxings, discs

Lam out of it

Get lost, leave, go away
"Why the hell don't you lam out of here,
bud? Before I throw a handful of fat
coppers in your lap."
From the novel *The Little Sister*,
Raymond Chandler, 1949

Lame

1. Something bad, poor quality, disappointing

2. "Can't understand, dumb, not able."
From the booklet *The Jives Of Doctor
Hepcat*, Lavada Durst, 1953

Lamps

Eyes
"I didn't think of anything but the blonde
in my arms, and the .45 in my fist, and
the twenty-six men outside, and the four
shares of Consolidated I'd bought that
afternoon, and the bet I'd made on the
fight with One-Lamp Louie, and the
defective brake-lining on my Olds, and
the bottle of rye in the bottom drawer of
my file cabinet back at Dudley Sledge,
Investigations."
Evan Hunter takes a sideswipe at Mickey
Spillane's tough-guy style. From the short
story *Kiss Me, Dudley*, 1954

Lamping

Looking or staring
"The customers were still lamping him
and the doll like they were fillum stars. To
one and all, such a drama could only
have one end. Outsize Romeo rescues
doll. Doll dates up. Nine months, she has
a lil baby goil to match."

	From the novel *Crooked Coffins* by Griff, 1930s
Latch on	Become aware, understand
Late bright	Late in the evening
Later	1. Goodbye
	2. A putdown eg: "Later for that Lawrence walk music, buddy."
Lay it down	Speak your piece "When he laid it, wham! it stayed there ..." From the spoken word performance *The Nazz,* Lord Buckley, 1951
Lay it on me	Tell me, say what you've got to say, give it to me
Lay some hot iron	Dance really well
Laying track	Lying
Layout	Living quarters, residence "They lead us into Merilli's private apartment, which is a swanky layout." From the novel *Killers Don't Care*, Rod Callahan, 1950
Lead poisoning	Getting shot
Leaky	Prone to tears "'She's a little red around the eyes.' 'Oh, Christopher, a weeper. If there's anything I hate, it's a leaky dame.'" The wives get bitchy about a newcomer, from the film *Orchestra Wives*, 1942
Let it hang	Wait a minute, hold on
Let me wake you, Jack	Let me put you straight, let me tell you something

Let's brush it hard and see where the dandruff falls	Let's discuss this carefully From the novel *Murderer's Row,* Donald Hamilton, 1962
Let's flat git it	Let's get real gone, let's go wild
Let's get out of the wheatfields, Mabel, we're going against the grain	Dean Martin alfresco at The Sands, Las Vegas, February 1964
Let's keep the dead leaves off the lawn	There's no use dragging up old arguments
Let's tear	Let's get in the car and drive fast
Let's you and me nibble one	Would you like a drink? From the novel *Farewell My Lovely,* Raymond Chandler, 1940
Letting the air out of someone	Stabbing them
Lick	"A hot phrase in rhythm." From *Down Beat's Yearbook of Swing,* 1939
Lid	Head, brain eg: "Stash that idea in your lid, dad . . ."
Lift the dogs	Pick your feet up, get a move on "Lift the dogs, Janson . . . we ain't got all night." From the novel *Chicago Chick*, Hank Janson, 1962
Like a rough night on the ocean	The worse for wear, bedraggled, not at your best "He found himself feeling sorry for the broad. She really looked like a rough night on the ocean." From the novel *Naked In Vegas*, John Denton, 1962
Lip locking	Kissing

121

Liquid grocery	Store selling alcohol
Liquorice stick	Clarinet
Line your flue	Eat From the autobiography *Really The Blues*, Mezz Mezzrow and Bernard Wolfe, 1946
Living end	1. The best, superlative, righteous
	2. The last straw, the limit "Christ, he thought. This was the goddam living end. The kid in hot water again. Molly wise to Irene. He was sick and tired of the whole stinking rat race." From the novel *Run Tough, Run Hard*, Carson Bingham, 1961
Loaded	1. Drunk or full of drugs "'What's the matter with you anyhow?' 'He's just loaded, honey . . .'" From the film *Rebel Without A Cause*, 1955
	2. Armed, packing a weapon, often written as loaded for bear "Both of them had a bulge on the right hip that meant just one thing. They were loaded." From the novel *Kiss Me, Deadly,* Mickey Spillane, 1953
	3. Rich, having plenty of money
Locoweed	Marijuana "He was raised on locoweed, He's what you call a Swing halfbreed." From the boogie-woogie recording *Cow Cow Boogie,* Ella Fitzgerald & The Ink Spots, 1946
Long bread	A large amount of money
Long gone daddy	In love, totally sent

"I'm a long gone daddy
And I'm long gone for you."
From the rockabilly recording *Long Gone
Daddy,* Pat Cupp & his Flying Saucers,
1956

Long goodbye   Death

Long green   A large amount of money

Longhairs   Highbrows, non-hipsters, squares,
fans of straight music
Down Beat's 1939 Yearbook of Swing
defines a longhair as "A symphony man,
one who likes classical music."

Look like Tarzan,   Little Richard's recipe for rock'n'roll
sing like Jane   success

Looker   A beautiful woman

Loose as a goose   Relaxed, at ease, intoxicated
See the jazz recording *Loose Like A
Goose*, Bennie Moten's Kansas City
Orchestra, 1929

Loose brains   Stupidity

Loose wig   Open-minded, receptive to new ideas

Lounge lizard   Sharp-dressed dude with an easy line in
patter

Louse up   Make a mistake

Lousemachine   Limousine

Lousy   1. Something rotten, low class, no good

   2. Full, replete, plentifully supplied
"The town's lousy with dames."
ie: There are lots of good-looking women
here.
From the novel *The Dead Don't Care*,
Jonathan Latimer, 1937

123

Lowdown	1. The full story, the inside dope
	2. Feeling blue, depressed
	3. Something treacherous or deceitful
Lower than a snake's belly	Depressed
Lower than the belly of a cockroach	Down, way down
Lubrication	Alcohol
Lug	Big guy, a heavyweight
Lunch hooks	Fingers
Lush	1. Alcoholic, heavy drinker "Never saw this motherless lush in my life before, Captain. Ain't them blood stains on his jacket?" From the novel *The Man With The Golden Arm,* Nelson Algren, 1949 For a suitably lurid pulp treatment of the evils of the demon booze, see the novel *The Lady Is A Lush*, Orrie Hitt, 1960 See the jazz recording *Nix On Those Lush Heads*, Blue Lu Barker with Danny Barker's Fly Cats,1939 "You crummy, one-eyed lush!" From the film *They Live By Night*, 1948 2. Good looking "A lush little miss said 'Come in, please.'" From *Saturday Night Fish Fry*, Louis Jordan & The Tympany Five, 1945
Lush dive	Cheap bar or gin joint
Lush hound	Drunkard

Main drag

Main street or thoroughfare
"I walked a couple blocks without sighting a bar, either on the main drag or the side streets."
From the novel *Savage Night*, Jim Thompson, 1953

Mainsqueeze

Girlfriend

Main stem

Main street or thoroughfare
In Horace McCoy's 1937 novel *No Pockets In A Shroud*, magazine editor Mike Dolan writes a regular column called *The Main Stem*.

Make

1. To see, to recognise

2. To seduce

Make a bulldog hug a hound

Very persuasive
"Big legged woman
Keep your dresses down,
You got somethin' baby
Would make a bulldog hug a hound."
From the Jerry Lee Lewis recording *Big Legged Woman*, 1958

Make like a fish

Have a bath

Make like a tree and leave

Quit the scene, take off, vamoose
"Well let's make like a tree and leave,
let's make like a storm and blow,
lets make like a chicken and fly this coop,
let's make like a rock and roll ..."
From the rockabilly recording *Make Like A Rock'n'Roll*, Don Woody, 1955

Make out like a foreign loan

To do well, be successful

Make the scene

1. To be there, to arrive or attend

	2. To comprehend the situation, to dig something
Make with a mouthful of Hi-Fi	Sing me a song
Make with the feet	Get moving, speed up, go away "On your way, dreamboat. Make with the feet." From the novel *The Little Sister*, Raymond Chandler, 1949
Making time	Becoming acquainted, necking, getting off with someone "Chuck would make time with any broad on my payroll. He's a young girl's dream, isn't he?" From the novel *Death Is Confidential*, Lawrence Lariar, 1959 "We were making good time, Getting in the know, When the captain said 'Son, we gotta go' I said 'That's alright, You go right ahead, I'm gonna Ubangi Stomp Till I roll over dead.'" From the rockabilly recording *Ubangi Stomp,* Warren Smith, 1956
Man	1. All-purpose hipster form of address 2. A policeman 3. Drug connection or supplier
Marble city	Cemetery
Mark	A victim, a sucker
Maryjane	1. Marijuana, or a marijuana user "'You know what a maryjane is? You know what a mainliner is?' 'I think so. Are you trying to tell me

these boys are drugged?'"
From the film *Touch Of Evil*, 1959

2. Lesbian
"'Your little Edie is a Mary Jane – a chicken for some dyke.'
'He means,' Stretch explained, 'a les-bi-an. A girl that likes girls.'"
From the novel *Twilight Girls*, Judson Grey, 1962

Maryjanes

Shoes
"My maryjane's been bitin' me for the past few minutes ... this one's bitin' my instep."
Frank Sinatra onstage at The Sands, Las Vegas, 1966

Mash

Alcohol
eg: "Drinkin' mash and talkin' trash."

Mash me a fin, gate, so I can cop me a fry

Lend me five dollars, I want to get my hair straightened

Mashed

Drunk, blasted, out of your gourd

Mason-Dixon line

Anywhere out of bounds when necking, smooching or parking and petting
See the jazz recording
That's Her Mason-Dixon Line,
Will Bradley & his Orchestra, 1941

Match me

Give me a light
"Match me, Sidney ..."
Burt Lancaster to Tony Curtis,
from the film *Sweet Smell of Success*, 1957

Mattress route

Sleeping your way to the top
"Gloria Clarke had made the big time by way of the mattress route. She was fruit for the newsmen, always hot copy ..."
From the novel *Death Is Confidential*, Lawrence Lariar, 1959

| **Max out** | To serve your entire prison sentence, with no parole |

| **Mazuma** | Money, the folding green |

| **Meal ticket** | 1. Job |
| | 2. Sugar daddy or benefactor |

| **Meat** | Blues slang for penis
"I'm going downtown
to old butcher Pete's,
cause I want a piece
of his good old meat ..."
From the blues recording *Take It Easy, Greasy,* Lil Johnson, 1936 |

| **Meat show** | Strip show, burlesque performance |

Meat wagon	1. Police vehicle
	2. Ambulance
	3. Hearse "There's your customer, everything else is for the meat wagon." Policeman to doctor after a shoot-out, from the film *Side Street*, 1950

| **Memphis umbrella** | A head full of serious hair grease or pomade, generally water-resistant |

Mess around	1. Have sex
	2. Dance "When I say git it, want you all to mess around ..." From *Pine Top's Boogie Woogie*, Pine Top Smith, 1928
	See also the blues recordings *That Dance Called Messin' Around,* Sara Martin, 1926 and *Messin' Around,* Trixie Smith, 1926

Mickey Finn	Knockout drug, usually disguised in an alcoholic drink
Midnight ramble	Late night show or dance Popular in blues circles during the 1920s.
Misery	1.Coffee "They's a jernt on Market Street belongs to a guy used to be a pal of mine in the field artillery. He'll set us up to coffee an'. He's a Greek, an' his misery's the hottest stuff in cups." From the novel *Somebody In Boots*, Nelson Algren, 1935 2. Gin
Miseries	The blues, depression "Sam, you sure do look like you've got the miseries." From the country recording *Lovesick Blues*, Emmett Miller & his Georgia Crackers, 1928 "Gonna tell Aunt Mary 'bout Uncle John, He claimed he had the miseries But he's havin' lots of fun ..." From the rock'n'roll recording *Long Tall Sally*, Little Richard, 1956
Mitt	Hand "No, buddy. No you won't. Keep your mitts off that desk." From the novel *Red Gardenias*, Jonathan Latimer, 1939
Mix it	To fight
Modernistic	With it, switched on, up to date See the jazz recording *You've Got To Be Modernistic*, Jimmy Johnson and Clarence Wilson, 1930
Moll	Girlfriend, usually tied up with a gangster Erika Zastrow wrote a story called *A Moll*

And Her Man for the September 1928 issue of *Black Mask* magazine, who billed it as "A romance of the Underworld".

Monday morning quarterback   Know-all, braggart

Moniker   Name

Mooch

1. An early jazz dance
The Edison company issued a recording by Collins And Harlan in 1914 called *Mootching Along*, accompanied by the following explanation:
"For a long time, way back in the days before the war, the negroes did a shuffling or lazy man's dance. They could do it for hours at a time without tiring. They called it The Mootch. The shuffle explains the movement of the feet, and the 'mootch' defines the lazy movement of the shoulders, and the sway and rhythm of the body."

"Professor Charles H. and Mrs. Anderson will present their latest ballroom dance *The Honolulu Mooch*, Saturday October 15th, 1915."
From an advert in the Harlem press, New York, 1915

See also the jazz recording *Shake It Up, Mooch It Up*, Eddie Heywood's Kansas City Blackbirds, 1927

2. To beg

3. To swindle or cheat
"Somebody said that Danny mooched Sam out of something like a hundred thousand bucks."
From the novel of the screenplay of *Ocean's Eleven*, George Clayton Johnson and Jack Golden Russell, 1960

4. To walk around aimlessly

130

Moocher Small time panhandler or beggar

Mooching the stem Begging on the street

Moo-juice Milk
From the autobiography *Really The Blues*, Mezz Mezzrow and Bernard Wolfe, 1946

Moonshine Bootleg hooch, usually made out in the hills

Moonshiner One who makes bootleg hooch
Early country star Fiddlin' John Carson, singer of classics such as *Who Bit The Wart Off Grandma's Nose* and *It's A Shame To Whip Your Wife On Sunday*, was described in a 1920s publicity handout as a "Moonshiner".

Moose-eyes A leering dude

More dough than an army baker Lots of money

More fun than a hot transfusion Really wild, the best, a knockout
"Well, crazy, you have just destroyed three thousand of my corpuscles
. . . Lady, you're more fun than a hot transfusion, you're really plasma. I think we could swing – if I knew the music."
Shell Scott talks that talk.
From the novel *The Kubla Khan Caper*, Richard S. Prather, 1966

Moss Hair

Most The best
"She got a lot
Of what they call the most."
From the rock'n'roll recording
The Girl Can't Help It, Little Richard, 1956

"Look, y'know, you could be the most, but all that old-style jive you got written up on the board is nowhere."
Gang leader J.I. talking to the teacher.
From the film *High School Confidential*, 1958

See also the vocal group recording *She's The Most*, The Five Keys, 1956

Most monster Mighty fine, the best

Motivate your piechopper Start talking

Motormouth One who talks a lot

Moth's chance in a nudist colony Doomed, no chance at all

Mothbox Piano

Mountain dew Bootleg liquor

Mouse 1. Black eye

2. Girl
"'A mouse I've never seen before saves me from the cops and asks me to a conference in her motel room. Would I walk in cold?'
She hesitated, and asked curiously,
'What's a mouse, Jim?'
'Don't act dumb. A mouse is a broad.'"
From the novel *Murderer's Row*, Donald Hamilton, 1962

Mouthpiece Lawyer
"'Polly, this is Morrie Tannenbaum, the famous criminal lawyer from Chicago . . .'
'Are you really a mouthpiece?' Polly demanded eagerly.'"
From the novel *The Deadly Lover*, Robert O. Saber, 1951

132

Mouthwash	Alcohol
Much beamy	Convivial, pleasant
Mudkicker	Prostitute, streetwalker
Muffin	Girl "That muffin you grifted – she's ok. Stuck her chin way out for you." From the film *Pickup On South Street*, 1953
Mug	1. Face, visage 2. A guy, a palooka, an ordinary Joe
Muggles	Marijuana
Mugshots	Photos in the police files of criminals' faces
Mugsnapper	Photographer
Mulligan stew	Cheap meal, poor man's food
Murderistic	Mighty fine See the jazz recording *Murderistic*, Jimmy Dorsey & his Orchestra, 1941
Mush	Sloppy sentiment "The world will pardon my mush but I have got a crush on you." From the live recording *I've Got A Crush On You*, Frank Sinatra, at The Sands, Las Vegas, 1966
Must have been tough on your mother, not having any children	I don't know what you are, but you don't impress me
Mutt	Dog
My finger's itching	Keep quiet or I'll shoot you

My meat, Jack	That's right up my street, that's the one for me
My solid pigeon, that drape is a killer-diller, an E-flat Dillinger, a bit of a fly thing all on one page	How to compliment a young lady on her new and pretty dress, according to Cab Calloway's Swingformation Bureau
My tonsils are dry	I'm thirsty, I could use a drink

Nab
Arrest
"You nabbed his brother on a narcotics rap."
From the film *Touch Of Evil*, 1959

Nabbers
Police, the forces of law

Naturally buzzin' cuzzin
A lively guy, a switched-on dude

Neck oil
Alcohol, booze

Necktie
The hangman's noose
"Well, they're gonna put a necktie on Gus he won't take off."
From the novel *Little Caesar*, W.R. Burnett, 1929

Necktie party
A lynching
"It sure looked as if I was about to be the guest of honour at a necktie party."
From the novel *Pop. 1280*, Jim Thompson, 1964

Nickel
Five year jail sentence

Nickel-nurser
Stingy, a tightwad

Nickel rat
Cheap crook
"'We've had twelve more legitimate citizen complaints against you this month, for assault and battery.'
'From who? Hoods, dusters, mugs – a lot of nickel rats.'"
Hands-on police work by the men of the 16th Precinct, from the film *Where The Sidewalk Ends*, 1950

Nighthawk
1. Taxi driver or cab

2. Late night person

See the jazz recording *Night Hawk Blues*, Coon-Sanders Original Night Hawk Orchestra,1924

See also the painting *Night Hawks,* Edward Hopper, 1942

Nix   No, nothing, no thanks

No bats allowed   "No ugly people invited (girls)."
Doctor Hepcat demonstrates his winning way with a party invitation. From the booklet *The Jives Of Doctor Hepcat*, Lavada Durst, 1953

No soap   No deal, nothing doing

Noggin   Brain
"'This dame,' I note, 'has got a noggin that works.'"
From the novel *Killers Don't Care*, Rod Callahan, 1950

No-goodnik from   A despicable person, a waste of space
Creepville   After the word Beatnik entered the language in the wake of the Russian Sputnik space mission, all kinds of slang words acquired similar endings.

"So the hell with Brett Sayers. Damn him to hell and gone. A no-goodnik from Creepville."
From the novel *Run Tough, Run Hard*, Carson Bingham, 1961

Noodle it out   Think it through, come to a conclusion

Nose candy   Cocaine
ie: In the novel *Dames Don't Care*, Peter Cheyney, 1937. However, in the short story *Dead Yellow Women*, Dashiell Hammett, 1920s, nose candy refers to heroin.

Nose paint   Alcohol

136

Not worth fifteen cents for parts	A loser, a nonentity, a worthless individual "I don't get it, Ed. Billy-Billy isn't anybody. He isn't worth fifteen cents for parts." From the novel *The Mercenaires*, Donald E. Westlake, 1960
Notch house	Brothel
Nothing shaking	No joy, nothing going on at all "Why must she be Such a doggone tease, There's nothing shaking But the leaves on the trees." From the rock'n'roll recording *Nothing Shaking (But the Leaves On The Trees)*, Eddie Fontaine, 1956
Now that you've laid me out, when you gonna bury me?	Have you finished criticizing me, or do I have to listen to more?
Now you're getting yourself some oxygen	Now you're talking, that's right
Nowhere	A failure, something worthless eg: "Man, that lame Pat Boone platter they're spinning is strictly nowhere."
Nuff sed	Need I say more, you can't argue with this At the Lincoln Theatre, Baltimore in November 1920, The Four Jolly Jassers were billed as "a real Creole Jass Band from the Land of Jazz, New Orleans – Nuff Sed".
Numbers racket	Illegal lottery based on numbers printed in the financial or sports pages of newspapers See the jazz recording *The Numbers Man*, Jack Sneed & his Sneezers, 1938

137

Off	To steal
Off the cob	Something corny
Oil merchant	A flatterer
On a roll	On a winning streak, lucky
On the beam	Intelligent, wise, alert

See the jazz recording *Theme On The Beam*, Lem Davis, 1946

"Well life is better
if you're on the beam,
and you dance to the rhythm
of your wash machine..."
From the rockabilly recording *Wash Machine Boogie*, Bill Browning & The Echo Valley Boys, 1956

"I had bought her a container of coffee on the way uptown, a sop to my concern about her. I wanted her on the beam." ie: I needed her to be thinking straight. From the novel *Death Is Confidential*, Lawrence Lariar, 1959

On the fly paper	Having your finger prints on file
On the Jersey side	On the wrong side, in the wrong place
On the lam	On the run from the law
On the sleeve	Habitually injecting drugs

"'I been on the sleeve since I got out of the army, Doc,' Frankie told him." From the novel *The Man With The Golden Arm*, Nelson Algren, 1949

On the take	Corrupt, accepting bribes

138

One bad stud	A hard guy, an evil dude See the vocal group recording *One Bad Stud,* The Honey Bears, 1954
One-in-a-bar and live forever	A bass player From *Down Beat's Yearbook of Swing,* 1939
One way ticket to Flipsville	Something mighty fine, really exciting
Onion ballad	A tearjerker, a sentimental song
Onion peeler	Switchblade knife
Only if you wanted to wear your face backwards for a while	Philip Marlowe tries to be reasonable, responding to a question with George Grosz's favourite tactic – a small yes and a big no. From the film version of *Farewell, My Lovely,* 1944, with Dick Powell as Marlowe.
Orphan paper	Rubber cheques, funny money, counterfeit currency
The other half of a half-wit	Stupid
Out on the roof	A night on the tiles "I was out on the roof last night and I've got a hangover like seven Swedes." From the novel *The Lady in the Lake,* Raymond Chandler, 1944
Out to the wide	Unconscious
Oversupply of mineral	Getting shot, being riddled with bullets "'The last guy who bought her a drink – they found him dead from an oversupply of mineral.' 'Mineral?' 'He had too much lead in his body.'" From the novel *Red Gardenias,* Jonathan Latimer, 1939

P.D.Q.

Pretty damn quick
"In the Holland box at the post office there's an envelope with my scrawl. In that envelope there's a parcel-room check for the bundle we got yesterday. Now get that bundle and bring it here P.D.Q."
Philip Marlowe telling his secretary how to pick up the black bird, from the film *The Maltese Falcon*, 1941

Pack, shack & stack

All your belongings – your clothes, your home, and your money

Pack your grip

Get your stuff together and go

Packing iron

Carrying a gun

Pad

1. Home, apartment, room
"You gotta have a date with me before you fall in my pad, darling ..."
From the novel *If He Hollers Let Him Go*, Chester Himes, 1945

2. To tell, to inform

Pad money

Rent money, as quoted in the street-gang study *Apaches Of New York*, A.H. Lewis, 1912

Pad your skull

Absorb information, learn things

Painting the town

Going out and having a wild night
"A smile on my face
A song on my lips,
Pretending is all I do.
I'm painting the town red
To hide a heart that's blue."
From the jazz recording
I'm Painting The Town Red,
Billie Holiday with Teddy Wilson
& his Orchestra, 1935

"There ain't no use, hanging round,
While you paint up the town.
Crazy me, learnin' slow,
Baby you sure got your man feelin' low."
From the country recording *Feelin' Low*,
Ernie Chaffin, 1956

Palomino   Good looking woman

Palooka   A mug, a punter, an ordinary joe
A disparaging term for a man, deriving
from a boxing term for a third rate
fighter.

Pan   Face
Hence the expression deadpan – showing
as much change of expression as a
corpse might.

Panel joint   Whorehouse where the rooms have slid-
ing panels so that the clients can be
robbed whilst otherwise engaged
"A panel joint is a fast shuffling clip. The
girl brings the sucker in. A bedroom, see?
They undress. She puts the sucker's pants
over a chair for him. While they're in
bed, a panel in the wall opens, and a guy
reaches in and frisks the sucker's pants."
From the novel *Little Men, Big World*,
W.R. Burnett, 1951

Panther piss   Bootleg liquor

Paper   A cheque

Paper hanging   Passing forged cheques

Park the hot boiler   Hide the stolen car

Park yourself   Sit down

Parking pet   Girlfriend

Parlour snake   Lounge lizard, smooth talker, oily
customer

"'Is that what the crowd does that keeps
following you around tonight?'
'What crowd,' she asked innocently.
'The fifty per cent of the sophomore class
that keeps following you around tonight?'
'A lot of parlour snakes,' she said
ungratefully."
From the short story *Josephine:
A Woman With A Past*, F.Scott
Fitzgerald, 1930

Paws	Hands
Peach	Good looking "A peach, a plum, a reg'lar steamer!" From the novel *Night Club Moll*, Nick Baroni, 1930s
Pearl diver	Someone who washes dishes
Pedal extremities	Feet See the jazz recording *Your Feet's Too Big*, Fats Waller & his Rhythm, 1941
Peel the ears and get it	Listen closely
Peeper	Private detective
Peg out	Die
Pegs	1. Legs 2. Trousers
Pen	Prison, penitentiary
Perforate	Shoot
Peter	A safe
Peterman	A safecracker
Picking iron out of your liver	Having gunshot wounds "'Keep on riding me, they're gonna be

picking iron out of your liver.'
'The cheaper the crook, the gaudier the patter, huh?'"
From the film *The Maltese Falcon*, 1941

Picking them up and putting them down	1. Running 2. Dancing
Piece of change	Some money
Piechopper	Mouth
Pin	To observe, to notice
Pineapple	Hand grenade or bomb "Johnny stopped a pineapple." ie: The dude's blown to pieces. From the novel *Night Club Moll*, Nick Baroni, 1930s "Look at this dump – four pineapples tossed at us in two days..." From the film *The Public Enemy*, 1933 Paul Cain wrote a story called *Pineapple* for the March 1936 issue of *Black Mask* magazine.
Pinched	Arrested
Pine box parole	To die in prison
Pipe	Saxophone
Pitch a bitch	Complain
Plant you now, dig you later	Got to go now, see you later
Planted	Buried "If I need the stuff and don't have it, I'm dead. I'm not exaggerating. And if I get planted, you're sunk."

143

From the novel *Darling, It's Death*, Richard S. Prather, 1959

Plastered

Drunk, sluiced, oiled-up, loaded
See the jazz recording *Plastered In Paris*, Chauncey Morehouse & his Orchestra, 1938

Platters

Records, discs, waxings
"The platters that matter..."
Defined as "A phongraph record" by *Down Beat's Yearbook of Swing*, 1939

Black Mask magazine published a story set in the record industry in May 1949 by Fergus Truslow entitled *Pardon My Poison Platters*.

Play bedwarmer

Sleep with someone

Play the chill

Ignore someone

Plumbers

Hit men, hired killers
"The big boys just give a couple of the plumbers your address and that's it. If the first set of plumbers don't fix the leak, they send another set."
From the novel *Little Men, Big World*, W.R. Burnett, 1951

Plumbing

A trumpet

Poke in the snout

A punch in the nose

Poker pan

A straight face, expressionless

Pokey

Prison
"The sheriff caught him out with Jezebel, Threw poor Okie in the county jail..."
From the rockabilly recording *Okie's In The Pokey*, Jimmy Patton, 1956

See also the jazz recording *Pokey Joe*, Bob Skyles & his Skyrockets, 1940

Polluted	Drunk "'I've changed my mind' 'About what?' 'About getting crocked.' 'You mean you're going to get get crocked?' 'Absolutely pie-eyed. Polluted. I'm going to celebrate.'" From the novel *This Is Murder*, Erle Stanley Gardner, 1935
Pops	"A word of greeting between musicians." From *Down Beat's Yearbook of Swing*, 1939
Pouring on the coal	Stepping on the accelerator, driving fast
Pouring water on a drowning man	Cruel behaviour "I saw her one day with a big old pan, pouring ice cold water on a drowning man." From the rockabilly recording *Evil Eve*, Joe D. Gibson, 1957
Prayerbones	Knees
Preparing bait	Putting on makeup
Pressed stud	Well-dressed dude, a guy who's looking sharp
Pretzel	A French horn
Promote	1. Obtain, steal 2. Seduce "That monkey's been trying to promote me for months." From the novel *Red Gardenias*, Jonathan Latimer, 1939
Prowl-car	Police vehicle "He'd have called all the cops in all the counties, and there'd be even more prowl cars hunting me now."

145

From the novel *Always Leave 'Em Dying*, Richard S. Prather, 1961

Pruning your peach-fuzz

Shaving your face
A phrase used by the rock'n'roll DJ The Mad Daddy, who later had a song named after him on the album *Songs The Lord Taught Us*, The Cramps, 1980

Puff

"To ride, walk or fly."
From the booklet *The Jives Of Doctor Hepcat*, Lavada Durst, 1953

Puff down the stroll

Drive down the street

Pull a creep

Leave

Pull into the curb, Daddy-O, before your dreamboat becomes a battleship

This relationship is doing you no good, give it up

Pull up and squat

Have a seat, sit yourself down
"'Hi boys,' he said, and jerked a thumb to some chairs along the wall. 'Pull up and squat.'"
From the novel *The Lenient Beast*, Fredric Brown, 1957

Pulling a judas

Putting the finger on someone, becoming an informer

Pulling the Dutch act

Committing suicide
"A girl pulled the Dutch act ..."
From the novel *Vengeance Is Mine*, Mickey Spillane, 1951

Pump

Heart
"'What happened?'
'Got him right through the pump with this.'
'It's a Webley. English, isn't it?'"
From the film *The Maltese Falcon*, 1941

146

Punk	Cheap crook, loser, mug
	Philip Ketchum wrote a story for the January 1950 issue of *Black Mask* magazine called *One Sunk Punk*.
Push-note	One dollar bill
Pushed	Killed, assassinated, knocked off
Puss	Face
	"Ludco's rat-like puss twisted into a grin." From the novel *Night Club Moll*, Nick Baroni, 1930s
	"My folks were tough. When I was born they took one look at this puss of mine and told me to get lost." From the film *The Hitch Hiker*, 1953
Put an egg on your shoe and beat it	Go away, get lost
Put on the feedbag	To eat
	"Say, Daddy-O, do you know where a cat can have a ball and put on a fine feedbag?" From the jazz recording *Two Blocks Down, Turn To The Left*, Cab Calloway & his Orchestra, 1930s
Put some alcohol in the radiator	Have a drink to warm yourself up
	"It's a cold night. Let's put some alcohol in the radiator." From the novel *Savage Streets*, William P. McGivern, 1959
Put that in writing and I'll paste it in my scrapbook	I don't believe you
	"'I like you, Johnny O'Clock.' 'Put that in writing and I'll paste it in my scrapbook.' 'I mean it ...'" From the film *Johnny O'Clock*, 1947
Put the bite on someone	1. Blackmail, extort money

2. Borrow money

Put the polish on the furniture
Sort yourself out, reach the optimum level
"One little shot of bourbon to put the polish on the furniture."
From the novel *Your Deal My Lovely*, Peter Cheyney, 1941

Put to bed with a shovel
1. Buried

2. Totally drunk

Putdown
Derogatory comment or criticism

Putting it down
Speaking, expressing an opinion
"I'm telling you what's being put down, you better pick up on it . . ."
From *Beware, Brother, Beware*, Louis Jordan & The Tympany Five, 1946

"I'm putting it down, but you ain't picking it up."
From *High School Confidential*, 1958

Putting on the dog
Pretending to be better than you are, putting on airs
"'These three birds came in on the Memphis train. Said they was with the T.V.A., but I'd bet dollars to doughnuts they wasn't.'
'What makes you think so?'
'I don't know. They never looked right somehow.'
'Well, that's the world for you,' Sybil said philosophically. 'People always putting on the dog, trying to act like they're you-know-what on a stick.'"
From the novel *Violent Saturday*, W.L. Heath, 1955

Putting on the style
Dressing suavely, going upmarket, having pretensions
"You were mine for just a while
Now you're putting on the style

And you've never once looked back
At your home across the tracks."
From the country recording
Pick Me Up On Your Way Down,
Charlie Walker, 1958

Putting up paper
for yourself

Bragging, singing your own praises
The reference is to running around town
sticking up posters with your own face on
them.

Q

Q

San Quentin prison
"She would be very nice to come home
to after a stretch in Q."
From the novel of the screenplay of
Ocean's Eleven, George Clayton Johnson
and Jack Golden Russell, 1960

Q.T.

1. Secret
eg: "Strictly hush hush, and on the Q.T."
ie: On the quiet, just between you and
me.
"You understand this is to be strictly
on the Q.T.?"
From the novel *The Glass Key*,
Dashiell Hammett, 1931

"You thought your little romance
was on the strict Q.T.,
so if you want your freedom P.D.Q.,
divorce me C.O.D."
From the country recording *Divorce Me
C.O.D.*, Merle Travis, 1946

2. "Cutie" – a slang term for a prostitute

Quail

Woman, girl
"'I say, Professor, you've hunted in all
parts of the country. What kind of quail
is that there, over there by the tree?'
'That is very unusual, Doctor. That kind
of game is not typical in this section.'
'What would you say it was, Professor – a
red-billed roadrunner?'
'No, no, no, Doctor, why I could say with
perfect confidence that's it's a black-
topped cinch . . .'"
Glen Miller's band get frisky,
from the film *Orchestra Wives*, 1942

R

Rack 'em back   Pull up the covers and go to sleep

Racket   Criminal enterprise, scam, business

Ragtop   Convertible car

Railroaded   Framed, fitted up on false evidence

Raise sand   Make a fuss, create a stir
"You're always raising sand baby,
and you're always doggin' me,
I believe to my soul,
you was stealin' back to your used-to-be."
From the blues recording *Two-Timin'*
Woman, Casey Bill Weldon, 1936

Rap   Criminal charge

Rap sheet   Criminal record
Blackie Audett, a bank robber who
worked with Dillinger, Baby Face Nelson
and Capone, published an autobiography
in 1955 called *Rap Sheet*.

Rat fink   A louse, a lowdown dog
"I got the word for you
Because that's what you is,
You is a rat fink,
You is a rat fink ..."
From the rock'n'roll recording
Rat Pfink A Boo Boo Theme,
Ron Haydock & The Boppers, 1966

Rat someone out   Betray, sell someone down the river,
inform on them

Rattler   Streetcar

Raw deal   Unfair break, tough shake of the dice
"Well I done had my last raw deal,
Baby I'm through with you ..."

From the rockabilly recording *Raw Deal*,
Junior Thompson & The Meteors, 1956

Read 'em and weep   What do you think of that, I've won,
I've beaten you

Ready   Hep, alert, knowing, aware of the scene

Real gone   1. Far out, wild, uninhibited, totally sent
"Hold it fellas,
That don't move me,
Let's get real, real gone for a
change ..."
The Hillbilly Cat puts a 50,000 volts up
the blues and winds up with rockabilly.
From *Milk-Cow Blues Boogie,*
Elvis Presley, 1955

2. Insane
"You're a schizo, and real gone."
Shell Scott receives some psychiatric
advice, from the novel *Always Leave 'Em
Dying*, Richard S. Prather, 1961

Real wild child   Hip, gone, a righteous groover
"Well I'm just out of school
Like I'm real, real cool,
I've got to jump, got to jive,
Got the message I'm alive,
I'm a wild, I'm a wild one,
Ooh yeah I'm a wild one.
I'm gonna keep a shakin'
I'm gonna keep-a movin' baby
Don't you cramp my style
I'm a real wild child."
From the rock'n'roll recording *Real Wild
Child*, Jerry Lee Lewis, 1958
(Originally by Australian rocker Johnny
O'Keefe, and later a sizeable hit for Mr.
James Osterberg.)

Red hot and ready   Fired up, all set for a wild night
to moan

152

Red onion   Low drinking joint
Louis Armstrong's first recording outfit
when he left King Oliver's Band in 1924
was called The Red Onion Jazz Babies.

Reefer   Weed, grass, dope
"'Man, what's the matter with that cat
there?'
'Must be full o' reefers.'
'Full o' reefers?'
'Yeah man.'
'You mean that cat's high?'
'Sailin' . . .'"
From *Reefer Man*, Cab Calloway, 1932

Harlan Lattimore & his Connie's Inn
Orchestra also recorded this tune in 1932,
with *Chant of the Weed* on the flipside.

Reet   Right, ok
See the jazz recording *Are You All Reet?*,
Cab Calloway & his Orchestra, 1941

Refrigerator   Prison

Repo man   Debt collector, someone who will come
round and repossess your car, your
home, etc

Rest the weight   Sit down, take it easy
"Rest the weight, Bob, you must be tired
of toting it around all day . . ."
From the novel *If He Hollers Let Him
Go*, Chester Himes, 1945

Rewire job   Medical attention
"They gotta doc here.
They're gonna rewire Crazy."
From the film *The Wild One*, 1954

Rhino   Money
"Give me my rhino instead of lip and
I'll pull my freight." ie: give me my
money instead of just talking and I'll
be gone.

From the short story *The Big Knockover*, Dashiell Hammett, 1920s

Ricky-tick Corny music, or anything clichéd

Riding academy Whorehouse

Riding for a fall In for trouble, taking chances

Riding herd Being in charge

Riding rubber Travelling by car

Riding the blinds Hopping a freight, hitching a ride at the end of a baggage car on a train
See *I'm Ridin' The Blinds On A West Bound Train*, Frank Marvin, 1930

Right guy Trustworthy, dependable
"I came here with a straight proposition, take it or leave it, one right guy to another."
From the film *The Big Sleep*, 1946

Righteous Cool, hip, in the groove and generally suave as all hell

Righteous bush Marijuana
From the autobiography *Really The Blues*, Mezz Mezzrow and Bernard Wolfe, 1946

Ripe for the lilies Dead

Roach Marijuana cigarette, joint, reefer

Roach bender Marijuana smoker

Roach killers Shoes

Roadhouse Lowdown roadside bar, outside city limits, often with a sleazy reputation
"They went further out on the highway to Buster's Roadhouse where chorus girls

wore small panties. There were rooms to rent by the hour in the attached motel behind."
From the novel *Go, Man, Go!,* Edward De Roo, 1959

See the jazz recording *Roadhouse Blues,* George Williams, 1926
(The flip was called *Bootlegging Daddy.*)

Rock and roll Sex
See the blues recording
My Man Rocks Me (With One Steady Roll), Trixie Smith, 1922

"If you wanna satisfy my soul,
Come on and rock me with a steady roll."
From the blues recording
You've Got To Save That Thing,
Ora Alexander, 1931

"Want you to roll me baby,
Like a baker rolls his dough,
Reel and rock and roll me,
Baby all night long."
From the blues recording *Rollin' Mama Blues,* Ruby Glaze & Hot Shot Willie (Blind Willie McTell), 1931

"Gonna hold my baby as tight as I can,
Tonight she'll know I'm a mighty man . . ."
From *Good Rocking Tonight,*
Roy Brown, 1946

See also (among many others) the blues recordings *Rock, Jenny, Rock,*
The Georgia Strutters, 1926; *Rocking And Rolling,* Robinson's Knights of Rest, 1930; *Rock It In Rhythm,* Tampa Red, 1938; *Rock And Rollin' Daddy,* Merline Johnson, 1939

Rock crusher Accordian

Rocket in your pocket	Erection "Let's go someplace Where we can rock a bit I got a rocket in my pocket And the fuse is lit." From the rockabilly recording *I Got A Rocket In My Pocket*, Jimmy Logsdon (aka Jimmy Lloyd), 1958
Rocks in your head	Stupidity
Rod	1. Gun "Turn around ... then shed your rod. Drop it on the floor." From the novel *The Fast Buck,* James Hadley Chase, 1952 2. Gunman "Two of the hottest rods in town combing the joints looking for you and you don't even get bothered enough to stop eating." From the novel *Kiss Me, Deadly*, Mickey Spillane, 1953 3. Car, short for Hot Rod
Rod merchant	Gunman
Rodded	Armed, carrying a gun
Roll them bones	Roll the dice "We're gonna pick 'em up an' shake 'em up 'An let 'em roll, All night long we're gonna roll them bones ..." From the rockabilly recording *Pick 'Em Up 'An Shake 'Em Up*, Cecil McCulloch & The Border Boys, 1956
Roll with the punches	Go along with things, accept the inevitable

Rooked   Cheated

Roost   Dwelling place, abode
1940s New York jazz venue The Royal
Roost was also know as the Metropolitan
Bopera House.

Roscoe   Handgun, firearm
"He propositions me we should heist the
Jitney Jungle and I axes him where we
can get a couple of rods, and he says we
oney need one, Homer, and I got that,
and he pull a roscoe off his hip."
From the short story collection
The Neon Wilderness, Nelson Algren,
1947

Rough-house   A fight or disturbance

Rubdown   A beating

Rub-joint   A cheap dancehall where dancing
partners can be hired

Rubbed out   Killed
"'Five thousand bucks for rubbing out a
horse.'
'Ok, Pops, how do I get it?'"
From the film *The Killing*, 1956

Rubber   Automotive transportation
"You still on rubber?"
ie: Do you still have a car?
From the novel *If He Hollers, Let Him
Go*, Chester Himes, 1945

Rubbernecker   Tourist, out-of-towner gawking at the
sights or anyone who stares
"'I saw you giving Peter March the glad-
eye.'
She said, 'You were rubbering at Carmel,
too ...'"
From the novel *Red Gardenias*,
Jonathan Latimer, 1939

Rube	A sucker, a hayseed, an easy mark
Rug	1. Hair "I've got to pick up on a barber because my rug needs much dusting." ie: I need a good haircut. From the booklet *The Jives Of Doctor Hepcat*, Lavada Durst, 1953 2. Dancefloor – as in *cutting some rug*
Rumble	1 Fight, especially a gang fight 2. A rumour, information "I'd like to know if it shows up. You're in a position where you should catch the rumble, maybe, and if you do, let me know fast." From the novel *Darling, It's Death*, Richard S. Prather, 1959
Run your mouth	Talk a lot See the jazz recording *You Run Your Mouth, I'll Run My Business*, Louis Armstrong, 1933
Running around	Being unfaithful, painting the town
Rupture head	Idiot, someone who's lost it completely

Sack	Bed
Sacked out	Asleep
Sacktime	Bedtime
Sailin'	High on drugs
Same old same old	Habitual, the daily grind
San Quentin quail	Underage girl, the kind that can land you in prison Dale Clark wrote a story called *San Quentin Quail* for the October 1941 issue of *Black Mask* magazine.
Sap	1. Fool, fall guy eg: "Stop playing me for a sap." 2. Cosh
Satchel mouth	A wide mouth Nickname for Louis 'Satchmo' Armstrong. See also the jazz recording *Satchel Mouth Baby*, The Four Jumps Of Jive, 1946
Saturday night special	Home-made or cheap handgun
Sauce	Alcohol, booze
Saucehound	Drunkard
Saucing a little on the much side	Getting drunk
Savvy	1. Knowledge, intelligence "Jim Thompson was pure American writing at its best ... He had more pistolero savvy than all the so-called great

159

American writers."
Harlan Ellison with some words of advice
for college lecturers.

2. Do you understand me?

Sawbox   A cello

Sawbuck   Ten dollars
               See the jazz recording *(I Found a)
               Sawbuck*, Johnny Crawford & his
               Orchestra, 1949

Scarf   1. To eat

               2. Food

Scat   1. Go away, get lost
               "'Shoo,' she said. 'Bon voyage. Scat.
               Scram. Goodbye. Yes?'"
               From the novel *The Icepick In Ollie
               Birk*, Eunice Sudak, 1966

               2. Whiskey

               3. Jazz singing using sounds instead of
               words
               A scat singer is defined by *Down Beat's
               Yearbook of Swing,* 1939, as a "Vocalist
               who sings rhythmically, but without using
               accepted English words."

               "Louis (Armstrong) first got me freed up
               from straight lyrics to try scatting ... I
               don't know how it got started, really, the
               scat singing. I think one night in the
               Cotton Club I just forgot the words to a
               song and started to scat to keep the song
               going. It was 1931."
               Cab Calloway, from his autobiography
               Of Minnie The Moocher And Me, 1976.
               Cab recorded a jazz tune called *Scat
               Song* in 1932.

               A fine example of scat being used in a
               song title would be the jazz recording

Wham (Re-Bop-Boom-Bam) by Doctor Sausage & his Five Pork Chops, which was made available to a suitably appreciative public back in 1940.

Jazz singer Scatman Crothers, in the latter part of his career, provided one of the voices for the film *The Aristocats*, before meeting a horrible end as a character in Stanley Kubrick's *The Shining*.

Scatter gun	A sawn-off shotgun
Schmo from Kokomo	An idiot, a square
Scoff	Food
Scram	Leave in a hurry, blow the joint
Scran	Food
The scramble egg treatment	Sex show "Ah yes, this joint I am familiar with. They do the scramble egg treatment on the floor to the delight of all onlookers." From the novel *Dig A Dead Doll*, G.G. Fickling 1960
Scratch	1. Kill someone 2. Money 3. To write
Scratched from the big race	To die
Scream sheet	Newspaper
Screaming mimis	Bad reaction to drugs, or withdrawal symptoms From the novel *The Screaming Mimi*, by Fredric Brown, 1956. Also filmed under the same title, 1958

161

Screw it on	Open up the throttle, cut loose
Screw up	Make a mistake
Screwed, blued and tattooed	A wild night out
Selling a bill of goods	Swindling someone, lying, conning "When we come around by the platform again I saw Socks and Rocky talking earnestly to Vic Lovell and Mary Hawley, Couple No. 71. 'Looks like Socks is selling her a bill of goods,' Gloria said. 'That Hawley horse couldn't get in out of the rain.'" From the novel *They Shoot Horses, Don't They?*, Horace McCoy, 1935
Send	1. To thrill, enrapture and generally fry the wig *Down Beat's Yearbook of Swing*, 1939, rather narrowly defined it as "To arouse the emotions with Swing music." 2. To smoke marijuana
Seven come eleven	A dice player's expression calling for good luck See the jazz recording *Seven Come Eleven*, Benny Goodman Sextet, 1939
Sew up your mouth	Shut up
Sex appeal	Falsies
Shack up	1. Live with, cohabit "Nothing could be finer than to shack up with a minor ..." Dean Martin, onstage at The Sands, Las Vegas, February 1964 2. To live somewhere "Just so happens I know where he's shacked up."

From the film *Pickup On South Street*, 1953

Shag

1. "A form of dance inspired by Swing music ..."
From *Down Beat's Yearbook of Swing*, 1939

2. To tail or follow someone
"Mrs Delancy is shagging a woman who was sitting next to Deirdre ..."
From the novel *Murder On Monday*, Robert Patrick Wilmot, 1952

Shake a leg

Get moving

Shake a tail feather

A dance which involves waving your hind quarters around in what some guardians of youthful morals would take to be a shameless and lascivious fashion
See the vocal group recording *Shake A Tail Feather*, The Five Du-Tones, 1963

Shake, rattle & roll

Having a wild time, originally specifically sexual
A show called *Shake, Rattle & Roll* ran at the Lafayette Theatre in Harlem in 1927 "with a Cast of Fifty Noted Colored Entertainers".

See also the jazz recording *Shake, Rattle & Roll,* Charlie Barnet & his Orchestra, 1940

Shake that thing

Dance
"When I say git it,
I want you to shake that thing ..."
From the boogie-woogie recording
Pine Top's Boogie Woogie,
Pine Top Smith, 1928

Shake the lead out of your shorts

Get moving, hurry up

Shake till the meat comes off the bones	Dance yourself ragged, strut your stuff
Shake your business up and pour it	Say what's on your mind
Shake your feet	Dance
Shaking two nickels together	Broke, down on your luck "I've been shaking two nickels together for a month, trying to get them to mate." From the novel *The Big Sleep*, Raymond Chandler, 1939
Shakedown	1. Swindle, confidence trick, robbery, extortion "But it'd serve that pokey right if somebody slapped him silly. He's been shaking down the greenhorns in here fouteen years." From the novel *The Man With The Golden Arm*, Nelson Algren, 1949 See the jazz recording *Honey Don't You Shake Me Down*, The New Orleans Jazz Band, 1924 2. Police search
Shamus	Private detective
Sharp as a tack	1.Well-dressed, stylish 2. Intelligent, clued-up in the wig department See the jazz recording *Sharp As A Tack*, Harry James & his Orchestra, 1941
Sharp enough to shave	Well dressed, stylish
She's my witch	She's my girlfriend "Artie swung to confront Rick. 'You better blow,' he said stiffly. He jerked a

thumb at Pat. 'This is my witch.'
'Was, you mean,' Pat said loudly. 'I told you nobody orders me around.'"
From the short story *A Hood Is Born*, Richard Deming, 1959

"Got hair as black as night
Got a skirt that's ooh, so tight,
Tellin' you I've got an itch
She's my witch."
From the rock'n'roll recording *She's My Witch*, Kip Tyler & The Flips, 1959

Sheik Boyfriend

Shill 1. Someone in league with a card sharp who helps to swindle other players by pretending to be an innocent participant in the game
"She's a shill for a gambler and she's got her hooks into a rich man's pup."
From the short story *Trouble Is My Business,* Raymond Chandler, published in *Dime Dectective* magazine, August 1939

2. Police baton

Shimmy Shaking, suggestive dance, supposedly originated by the performer Little Egypt at the 1893 Chicago World's Fair
See the jazz recording *I Wish I Could Shimmy Like My Sister Kate,* The Cotton Pickers, 1922

Shiv Small knife for stabbing people, sometimes home-made
"'Let's see the shiv,' he said.
'The what?'
'The pig-sticker, the switchblade, the knife, for Christ's sake. Don't you under-stand English?'"
From the novel *Savage Night*, Jim Thompson, 1953

165

Shoo-in	A dead cert, bound to win
Shoot the sherbert to me, Herbert	Give me a shot of booze Also Slip the juice to me, Bruce, and Pour a gallon in me, Alan
Shoot the works	Spill the beans, tell all
Shoot your cookies	Vomit "You better go lay down somewhere, buddy. If I'm any judge of colour, you're goin' to shoot your cookies." From the short story *Finger Man*, Raymond Chandler, 1934
Shooting a line	Lying, telling a fanciful story
Short	An automobile "Your fly chick is looking most frantic and your short is all gassed up and ready to roll." From the booklet *The Jives Of Doctor Hepcat*, Lavada Durst, 1953
Short con	Short term confidence trick
Shot all to hell	Worn out, broken, destroyed
Shot-rodder	Someone who's lost it, a crazy guy, a mess
Shove in your clutch	Get moving, get on with it
Shovel city	To like something, ie: to dig it
Showcasing	Showing off, bragging
Shower down	Empty your pockets
Shroud-tailor	Undertaker
Shuck & jive	Mess around, waste time
Shucker	Stripper, burlesque dancer

166

Shutterbug	Photographer
Sidekick	Follower, pal, flunky
Sideman	Musician in a band, but not the leader of the band
Sides	Records
Sing	Confess, spill the beans
Sinhound	A priest
Sissy gun	Small calibre weapon
Sister	Dame, doll, etc "She's a first-class four flushin' double dealin' twicin' sister of Satan who would take a sleepin' man for the gold stoppin' in his right-hand eye tooth." From the novel *Dames Don't Care*, Peter Cheyney, 1937
Six-gun payoff	Death, getting shot "You saw a nice way to drop it in my lap and promised the two witnesses a six-gun payoff unless they saw it your way." From the novel *Vengeance Is Mine*, Mickey Spillane, 1951
Sixty minute man	Lover with staying power "Looky here girls I'm telling you now they call me Lovin' Dan, I rock 'em, roll 'em all night long, I'm a sixty minute man . . ." From the vocal group recording *Sixty Minute Man,* Billy Ward & The Dominoes, 1950
Sizzler	The electric chair
Ski ride	Cocaine binge
Skin beater	Drummer

167

Skin show	Striptease performance
Skinny	Information, hot news
Skins	A kit of drums
Skull orchard	Cemetery
Skull work	Thinking
Sky-pilot	Preacher
Slammer	Prison
Slap happy	Keen, possibly over-enthusiastic "He's a slap-happy bird with a gun." From the film *The Devil Thumbs A Ride*, 1947
Slaughter in the pan	Beefsteak
Slave	A job, employment
Slay me now, I don't want to go another further	I'm having a really good time
Slinky piece of homework	Good looking woman "She's a slinky piece of homework with auburn hair and green eyes. She's wearing a low cut dress of shimmering black which clings seductively to her ripe curves. Me, I get a thrill just looking at her." From the novel *Killers Don't Care*, Rod Callahan, 1950
Slip him the boodle	Give him the money
Slip him the dose	Shoot him
Slipped disc party	A house hop with the wildest waxings "'You goin' to Norma's, Eliz? It's a slipped disc party.'

'Will do, Mildew.'
I said 'I don't want to be an old square,
but what's a slipped disc party?'
'Discs are platters, you know, records,
and slipped means, well, you're out of
this world, slipped over the edge.'"
From the novel *Drive East On 66*,
Richard Wormser, 1962

Slop   Food

Sloppy drunk

Soused, smashed, juiced to the gills
See the jazz recording *Sloppy Drunk
Woman*, Blue Chip Norridge Mayhams &
his Blue Boys, 1936

"Down in New Orleans where
everything's fine
All them catfish drinkin' that wine,
Drinkin' that mess is pure delight,
Get sloppy drunk and start fightin' all
night ..."
From the R&B recording
Drinkin' Wine Spo-Dee-O-Dee,
Stick McGhee, 1949

**Slower than
molasses in
January**

Not very bright, not quick on the
uptake

Slug

1. A bullet
"'Shut up, you squealer!' Baird exclaimed.
'We're both in this! You try and walk out
on me and I'll put a slug into you!'"
From the novel *The Fast Buck*,
James Hadley Chase, 1952

2. A punch
"'Orlik?' he sniffed, checking it against
his memory. 'Not the big shot? Last time
I read the name, he slugged a guy in a
city club. Right?'"
From the novel *Death Is Confidential*,
Lawrence Lariar, 1959

3. A dollar

169

4. A shot of booze
"She gets a few slugs under her girdle
and she thinks it's Christmas."
From the novel *Red Gardenias*,
Jonathan Latimer, 1939

Slush pump A trombone

A smack in the face with a steam shovel A punch in the mouth

Smart up in the top storey Intelligent

Smeller Nose

Smooching party Kissing

Snatch Kidnapping

Sneaky Pete Cheap wine

Sniffing Arizona perfume Going to the gas chamber

Snort A drink
"Come on over to Plunkett's and
we'll have a snort on it."
From the novel *Blow Up A Storm*,
Garson Kanin 1959

Snow Cocaine

Snow job A misleading story, a pack of lies
designed to divert attention from the real
situation

Snowbird Cokehead
"My mother sells snow to the snowbirds,
my father makes barbershop gin,
my sister sells jazz for a living,
and that's why the money rolls in."
Jail song from the film *The Young
Savages*, 1960

So long Pal, be pure — Hipster farewell

So mean you won't even spend a weekend — Stingy, a tightwad

So round, so firm, so fully packed — Good looking
See the country recording *So Round, So Firm, So Fully Packed*, Merle Travis, 1947

Soak your face — Get drunk

Sob sister — Sad, crying, miserable

Sob story — Hard-luck tale, depressing story

Sock —
1. Close dancing
"'. . . would you mind, you're dancing too close.'
Lover grinned. 'Don't like to sock it in, huh?'
'Why get ourselves all excited?' Mary said, looking at him coolly now. 'It's too hot to raise a temperature.'"
From the novel *Tomboy*, Hal Ellson, 1952

2. Great, really good, outstanding

Sock hop — Teenage dance party

A sock on the button — A punch in the face

Sodom by the Sea — Coney Island

Soft money — Easy money

Solid — Good, in order, righteous
See the jazz recordings *Solid, Jack, Solid*, Ollie Shepard, 1938 and also *You're Solid With Me*, Lovin' Sam with the Burns Campbell Orchestra, 1938

171

"She never ever wants to go to sleep,
she says that everthing's solid
all-reet ..."
From the jazz recording *Who Put The
Benzedrine In Mrs. Murphy's Ovaltine?*,
Harry "The Hipster" Gibson, 1946

**Solid, Jack, I'll dig
you in your
den gradually**

The proper reply when invited to
someone's house for a visit, according
to Cab Calloway's Swingformation Bureau

Solid sender

A real knockout
Down Beat's Yearbook of Swing, 1939,
defined a sender as "1. A musician capable of playing good hot solos, and 2. A
performance that pleases Swing fans".

"Oh my Linda,
she's a solid sender,
you know you'd better surrender."
From the rock'n'roll recording *Slippin' &
Slidin'*, Little Richard, 1956

Roy Milton had an R&B group from
1946 to 1956 called the Solid Senders.

"Boy that man's a solid sender,
when he gets riding on that go-toy
the cats really start cryin'."
From the film *Orchestra Wives*, 1942

**Some dollars to
walk and wake up
with**

Spending money, working capital

Songbird

Female vocalist
At the Harlem's Lafayette Theatre in July
1919 the Five Dixie Girls were being
advertised as "A Quintette of Classy
Songbirds".

Sound

To listen
"Talk up, man, I don't sound you at
all ..."
From the film *High School Confidential*,
1958

172

Sounds	Music
Soup	1. High-performance hotrod fuel, a special mixture

2. Swearing
"Kicking him off the team for that little burst of soup, it wasn't fair. What did the coach have against him?"
From the novel *Scandal High*, Herbert O. Pruett, 1960

3: Explosives
"The two Cs got him. For that many pieces of paper he could take his chances with a gallon of soup."
ie: For that much money he'd risk being blown up.
From the novel *Kiss Me, Deadly*, Mickey Spillane, 1953

Sourpuss   Bad tempered, ugly

South of the slot   The wrong side of the tracks, the poor part of town, from humble beginnings

Southpaw   Left handed
See the boogie-woogie recording *Southpaw Serenade*, Will Bradley & his Orchestra with Freddie Slack on piano, 1942

South view   An interesting viewpoint
"I am tellin' you that the south view of this dame from the east when she is walkin' north would make a blind man turn to hard liquor."
From the novel *Your Deal, My Lovely*, Peter Cheyney, 1941

Soused   Drunk
"Poppa's gone up to town. He'll get himself soused and shoot his mouth off."
From the film *They Live By Night*, 1948

173

Sousepot	Drunkard
Spare me the hot air	Shut up, I'm not interested
Spigot bigot	Prohibitionist, anti-alcohol campaigner
Spill your guts	Confess, tell all, become an informer "Little Joe waggled the bottle admonishingly at his companion. 'You hadn't ought to have done that,' he said, 'just when he was going to spill his guts.'" From the novel *Headed For A Hearse*, Jonathan Latimer, 1935
Spinach	Dollar bills
Splinter your toupee	Go crazy, flip your wig
Split, no-tomorrow style	Leave in a great hurry
Splitting the freight on a crash-pad	Sharing the rent for an apartment
Sporting house	Brothel
Squeaking shoe leather	Walking around
Squall & ball & climb the wall	Have a wild time This was the catch-phrase of "Smilin'" Eddie Hill, 1940s country performer and DJ on WMC radio in Memphis.
Square a beef	Sort out a problem or a grievance "You couldn't square a beef with a stupe." ie: You can't settle an argument with an idiot. From the novel *The Grifters*, Jim Thompson, 1963
Square from Delaware	Unenlightened person See the jazz recordings *(You're A) Square From Delaware*,

Fats Waller & his Rhythm, 1940;
It's Square But It Rocks,
Count Basie & his Orchestra, 1941;
Serenade To A Square,
Sonny Stitt & The Be Bop Boys, 1946

Square meal on a round plate Food

Squawkers Parents
"Must be a lot of our squawkers could give a finger." ie: A lot of our parents could lend a hand.
From the film *Shake, Rattle And Rock*, 1957

Squeaker A violinist

Squeal Confess

Squealer Informer

Squirting metal Firing a gun

Stabbing heels High heels

Stacked Well built, a good figure
"She was stacked. She was pretty. She was just about everything you could want in a woman."
From the novel *Savage Night*, Jim Thompson, 1953

Stacked up A car crash
"'What happened?'
'I stacked it up,' Brad said slowly, looking her right in the eye. She blinked under his hard, level stare.
'You,' she said with a gasp. 'You stacked it up? You mean you had an accident?'"
From the novel *Run Tough, Run Hard,* Carson Bingham, 1961

Stagger-juice Alcohol
"This dame is plumb full of

175

stagger-juice."
From the novel *Dames Don't Care*,
Peter Cheyney, 1937

Stallion

Boyfriend, stud
"She's been tied in knots with so many stallions, no detective on earth could pick the right goon out of that mob in the restaurant."
From the novel *Death Is Confidential*,
Lawrence Lariar, 1959

Stand by while I pad your skull

Listen carefully

Stand-up guy

Reliable, helpful, good in a tight spot
"We'll probably never see each other again after we split up the money and break up tonight, but in my book you'll always be a stand-up guy."
From the film *The Killing*, 1956

Static

Complaints, noise
"Hey, that's enough static out of you."
Station cop to James Dean.
From the film *Rebel Without A Cause*,
1955

Stay cool, hang loose, admit nothing

Recommended behaviour when dealing with the forces of law and order

Steady as rain

Going steady, having a regular partner

Step-ins

Underwear

Step off

Be executed, killed by the State

Steppin'

Dancing

Steppin' on the gas

Literally, to drive fast, but also just to cut loose and get wild
See the jazz recording *Steppin' On The Gas*, Jimmy O'Bryant's Famous Original Washboard Band, 1925

Stewed to the gills	Drunk The Edison company put out a wax cylinder in 1913 with a comedy sketch called *Funny Doings At Sleepy Hollow*, in which one of the characters utters the line "I'm a little stewed, yer see …"
Stick	1. Reefer, joint See the jazz recording *Burnin' Sticks*, Toots Mondello & his Orchestra, 1939 2. Bar eg: "Behind the stick", where a barman stands.
Stick with me, you'll come in on the tide	I'll look after you "Stick with us kid, you'll come in on the tide." The chorus girls lend Ruby Keeler a hand, from the film *42nd Street*, 1933
Stiff	Corpse
Stiff one	A drink with a high alcohol content
Stinking	1. Completely drunk 2. Loaded with money
Stir	Prison
Stone	Complete, full
Stone college	Prison
Stoned	1. Drunk "I would say, roughly, that Dean Martin has been stoned more often than the United States embassies …" Frank Sinatra onstage at The Sands, Las Vegas, 1966 2. On drugs, particularly marijuana
Stool pigeon	Informer

Storage	Jail "Ah, maybe we better put this nut in storage." From the novel *Always Leave 'Em Dying*, Richard S. Prather, 1961
Stow it	Shut up
Stow the hot talk	Shut up
Straight dope	The truth, reliable information "Had The Man given me the straight dope? He might have . . ." From the novel *Savage Night*, Jim Thompson, 1953
Straight from the cookhouse	Inside information, a hot tip
Straight from the fridge	Cool "Great dad, great, straight from the fridge." From the film *Beat Girl*, 1960
Straight, no chaser	The undiluted truth, the real thing, reliable information Art Taylor put out a jazz track in 1959 called *Straight, No Chaser*.
Straighten up and fly right	Behave properly, do the decent thing, sort yourself out "'All right!' Schaeffer's voice was savage. He was the cop again. 'Do what you want. But for God's sake, Pop, come out of it. Straighten up and fly right.'" From the novel *Violent Night*, Whit Harrison, 1952 "Straighten up baby, Why don't you fly right sometimes, That will ease my temperature And cool my worried mind." From the blues recording *Straighten Up Baby*, James Cotton, 1954

Stretch	Prison sentence
Strictly for the birds	1. Useless, a pack of lies
	2. It's not for me, I'm not interested "'How do you like being a deputy G-Man, Janson?' 'It's crazy, man,' I told him. 'Real crazy. Strictly for the birds.'" ie: I don't like it. From the novel *Chicago Chick*, Hank Janson, 1962
Strictly union	Corny music, unadventurous
Stroll	The street
Struggle	Dance "Hey, how 'bout you? You wanna struggle?" From the film *The Wild One*, 1954
Struggle-buggy	Automobile See the jazz recording *Struggle Buggy*, King Oliver & his Orchestra, 1930
Strut yo' stuff	Dance, perform or otherwise show what you're made of A theatre production called *Strut Yo' Stuff*, billed as "A Stupendous Musical Satire", was running in New York in December 1920. See also the blues recording *Get Yourself A Monkey Man, And Make Him Strut his Stuff,* Butterbeans & Susie, 1924
Struttin'	Dancing See the blues recordings *I'm A Doggone Struttin' Fool,* Noble Sissle, 1921, and *Learn To Do The Strut,* Don Parker & his Orchestra, 1923
Stud	Guy, hepcat, dude "I'm set to drift when Elmo pops up with two other studs. Elmo's the President of

the mob, the boss cat. He's not too big,
but a rough stud when the chips are
down."
From the short story *The Rites Of
Death*, Hal Ellson, 1956

Stud dog	Sexually demanding, a bit of a caveman "She had tried to tell Sylvia that Willie-Joe was a stud dog." From the novel *Scandal High*, Herbert O. Pruett, 1960
Stuff with the dead ones' pictures	Paper money From the autobiography *Really The Blues*, Mezz Mezzrow and Bernard Wolfe, 1946
Suck the bottle	Drink, get drunk "Four bottles ... And you sucked up three of 'em. I had to practically clip you to get a swallow. You said your leg hurt 'an you wanted to get drunk." From the novel *Fast One*, Paul Cain, 1936
Sucker bait	Inducement, advertising
Sucker list	Client base, mailing list
Suds	Beer "'I was just thinking,' he said, 'how a nice beer would go right now. A nice, ice-cold suds with about an inch of cuff on it.'" From the novel *Violent Saturday*, W.L. Heath, 1955
Suitcase	A kit of drums
Suited down	Well dressed, sharp
Suppose we get together and split a herring	Would you like to go out with me one night?
Swapping chews	Kissing

180

Sweating out the rest of it	Serving a life sentence in the slammer
Sweet swingin' sphere	The world "I'm gonna put a cat on you that's the sweetest, gonest, wailingest cat that ever stomped on this sweet swingin' sphere . . ." From the spoken word recording *The Nazz*, Lord Buckley, 1951
A swell piece	Good looking woman
Swelling up like a poisoned pup	Pleased with yourself, conceited, proud
Swing	1. Term for jazz music that became popular from the very end of the 1920s *Down Beat's Yearbook of Swing*, 1939, defined the word as "The latest name for hot jazz music; more freely used as a term applied to all popular jazz". See the jazz recording *Swing, You Cats*, Louis Armstrong & his Orchestra, 1933 2. Mode of behaviour "'I don't know,' Frankie sympathized. 'It's just that some cats swing like that, I guess.'" From the novel *The Man With The Golden Arm*, Nelson Algren, 1949 3. Allegiance eg: "Which gang do you swing with?"
Swing shift	Evening work
Swingin'	Cool, crazy, in the groove, the best
Switching channels	Changing your story
Swooner	Someone good looking
Sympathy	"Let me put it this way – I should be

sincerely sorry to see my neighbour's children devoured by wolves."

Waldo Lydecker positively oozing sympathy.

From the film *Laura*, 1944

T

T.C.B. — Taking care of business – the personal motto of Elvis Presley

Tab-lifter — Nightclub customer

'T'aint no crack but a solid fact — It's the truth
From the autobiography *Really The Blues,* Mezz Mezzrow and Bernard Wolfe, 1946

Take a bite of air — Get lost

Take a raincheck — Pass up an opportunity

Take a run-out powder — Leave in a hurry
"He had too much to lose. Molly would peel him skinless if he ever decided to take a powder."
From the novel *Run Tough, Run Hard,* Carson Bingham, 1961

Take it on the lam — Run from the law

Take off your stomping shoes — Stop looking for trouble, calm down, I don't want a fight

Take some hot groceries — Eat a meal

Taken off the payroll — Killed, assassinated

Takes the paint off your deck — It's rough booze, strictly low class

Talking in dribbles — Speaking rubbish, making no sense

Talking that talk — Speaking in jive-talk, using hipster slang
See the vocal group recording *Talk That Talk,* The Du Droppers, 1955

Talking trash — Verbal abuse

183

Talking turkey	Straight talking, honesty
Tall	Drunk "'I think you are a splendid woman,' he said. 'I'm high, wide and handsome,' she said. 'I'm tall.' 'Tall?' 'High. Tight. Crocked. Drunk.'" From the novel *Red Gardenias*, Jonathan Latimer, 1939
Tamp on down the stroll	Walk down the street
Tank town	Small town, out in the sticks, the opposite of a big city like New York or Chicago "What's a fast guy like you doing at a tank-town teacher's college?" From the novel *Savage Night*, Jim Thompson, 1953
Tanked	Drunk
Tap the bottle	Drink
Tapped	Arrested
Tapping a jug	Robbing a bank "He blasted a couple of fuzz while he was tapping a jug." ie: He shot a couple of policemen when robbing a bank. From the novel *Murder On Monday*, Robert Patrick Wilmot, 1952
Tapsville	Broke
Taxi dancer	Paid dancing partner at a dancehall, not the most respectable of profession "'I can tell you where she works.' 'Where?' 'At the Clark-Erie ballroom. She's a host- ess there.' 'A taxi-dancer?'"

'I reckon that's what you calls 'em ...'"
From the novel *The Lady In The
Morgue*, Jonathan Latimer, 1936.

"Listen: it's a safe bet Baird's just
knocked off one of Rico's taxi-dancers."
From the novel *The Fast Buck,*
James Hadley Chase, 1952

Tea

Weed, marijuana
"I didn't know what was happening to
me, and I suddenly realized it was only the
tea that we were smoking; Dean had
bought some in New York. It made me
think that everything was about to arrive –
the moment when you know all
and everything is decided forever."
Sal Paradise grazes on some grass
From the novel *On The Road,*
Jack Kerouac, 1957

Tea hound

A marijuana smoker

**Tear it down, soup
it up, and strip
it for speed**

Sort it out, adapt things to suit your
own requirements

Teenage fluff

Young girl
From the novel *If He Hollers Let Him
Go*, Chester Himes, 1945

**Teeth and tongue
will get you hung**

You talk too much

Tell it like it is

Straight talking, telling the truth

**Tell that to a mule
and he'll kick your
head off**

That's a lie, I don't believe you

Terpsichorical

Dancing
"Hey baby, how's about you and me
getting terpsichorical? Let's go downstairs
and fly."
Oliver Reed invites a charming young

185

lady to dance, from the film *Beat Girl*,
1960

**That ain't second
base**

Watch where you're going
"Man, lookout where you're steppin'
That ain't second base."
From the boogie-woogie recording
Down The Road A Piece, Ray McKinley,
1942

**That chick is locked
up in this direction,
so just cut out while
your conk is all in
one portion**

"How you can tell someone to stop
annoying the young lady you are
escorting."
From Professor Cab Calloway's
Swingformation Bureau

**That don't move
me**

I'm not impressed
See the rockabilly recording *That Don't
Move Me*, Carl Perkins, 1956

**That gives me a
large charge**

I'm excited, I'm impressed

That thing

Sex organs
"My friend picked a new girl
in a little dance-hall
he used to be a high-stepper
but now he can't walk at all
somebody's been using that thing
somebody's been using that thing
just as sure as you're born
somebody's been using that thing."
From the blues recording
Somebody's Been Using That Thing,
The Hokum Boys, 1929

The phrase became something of an
obsession with blues songwriters of the
Twenties and Thirties, ie: *Shake That
Thing*, Ethel Waters, 1925; *I'm Wild
About That Thing*, Bessie Smith, 1928;
Let Me Pat That Thing, The Hohum
Boys, 1929; *Bury That Thing*, Roosevelt
Sykes, 1929; *It's A Pretty Little Thing*,
Tampa Red, 1930; *She's Dangerous*

With That Thing, Lonnie Johnson,
1931; and, on an educational note,
What's The Name Of That Thing?, The
Chatman Brothers, 1936

That vibrates me	I'm impressed, I really like it
That's a bringer, that's a hanger	That's a bringdown, that's a hangup, that's depressing See the jazz recording *That's A Bringer, That's A Hanger* Slim Gaillard & his Flat Foot Floogie Boys, 1939
That's a gas	1. That's great, that's really good 2. That's a laugh, what rubbish "Afraid of you? That's a gas! He could stamp you out like an ant. You're nothing to him." From the novel *Two Timing Tart*, John Davidson, 1961
That's a panic and a half	That's really amusing
The words don't go with the music	I don't believe you
Them's the breaks, kid	That's life
They threw babies out of the balcony	That performance went down a storm
They'll pat you with a spade	You're likely to get yourself killed "I got lead in this here rod and my finger's itching. One crack out of any of you and they'll pat you with a spade." Rico talks tough, from the novel *Little Caesar*, W.R. Burnett, 1929
Thin man	Non-existent person on the payroll, whose wages find their way into the pockets of the boss

Thinking room	Signs of intelligence in the face "Her eyes were wide set and there was thinking room between them." From the short story *Trouble Is My Business*, Raymond Chandler, 1939
Thinner than the gold on a weekend wedding ring	Extremely thin
Third degree	Heavy duty interrogation, often involving fists, clubs and other subtle methods of persuasion
This bird's gonna pull his freight	I'm leaving, I'm outta here
Thou shalt not bug thy neighbour	The hip commandment ie: Be cool, don't annoy people.
Threads	Clothes
Threaded down	Well dressed, sharply turned out
Three sheets to the wind	Drunk
Three singles or a large shakedown	Three single rooms or a suite?
Three time loser	Prisoner serving a life sentence after three convictions
Thrill up on the hill	Dance or party "There's a thrill up on the hill, let's go, let's go, let's go." From the R&B recording *Let's Go, Let's Go, Let's Go,* Hank Ballard, 1960
Throttle jockey	Hot-rodder
Throw that dirt in your face	Being buried "A guy's got a right to expect his family to show up when the time comes

to throw dirt in his face."
From the novel *Halo In Blood*, Howard
Browne, 1946

"I'll hire a black cadillac
To drive you to your grave
I'm gonna be there baby
Throw that dirt in your face
I'll wear a black mink coat
A diamond ring on my hand
Before they put you underground
I'll have myself another man . . ."
From the rock'n'roll recording, *Black
Cadillac* Joyce Green, 1956

Throwing lead

Shooting, firing guns
"Why, you bone-headed gazooma, you
ain't even got a mind o' your own. Okay,
so nobody knows him. That's fine. Maybe
tomorrow, the day after, some other
finger-man'll be up here throwin' lead
around. And to think I pay you guys
dough. Get the stiff dumped in the river.
And for Christ's sake put weights on the
feet."
Problems with the hired help, from the
novel *Hot Dames On Cold Slabs*,
Michael Storme, 1950

Thrush

Female singer

Thumb

Hipster handshake
"Hey Pops, thumb me will ya Daddy-o?"
From the film *The Wild One*, 1954

Tie one on

Get drunk

Tight as a vault with a busted timelock

Closed, impenetrable

Tighten someone's wig

Introduce them to marijuana

Tighteye

Sleep

Tijuana bible	Pornographic magazine
Till-tapper	Thief, store burglar
Tin ears strictly around the block	Unsophisticated people From the film *High School Confidential*, 1958
Tip-top daddy	Suave, in the groove, a righteous dude
Tip your hole card	Give the game away, reveal your intentions
Tip your mitt	See Tip your hole card
Toeology	Tapdancing eg: "An upstate guy wigs you with some most burnt toeology." ie: A hip dude impresses you with the skill of his tapdancing.
Togged to the bricks	Dressed up, sharply turned out, suave
Tomato	Good looking woman "Here was I in my own apartment with three beautiful tomatoes and all I could think of was getting rid of them. Life can be really cruel sometimes." From the short story *The Live Ones*, Richard S. Prather, 1956 "She's a real sad tomato, She's a busted valentine ..." Lauren Bacall's song from *The Big Sleep*, 1946 "Give a lift to a tomato, you expect her to be nice, don't you?" From the film *Detour*, 1945
Tonsil paint	Alcohol
Too lovely to feed to the hogs	Very attractive, good looking

Toots	1. Term of affection, eg: "Best take a shot, toots." ie: Have a drink, honey. Sometimes the word is spelt Tutz as in "How're you gettin' along with tutz?" From the novel *Red Gardenias*, Jonathan Latimer, 1939 2. Patronising or threatening term of address "'Watch your step, Toots,' he said evenly. 'I shan't tell you again.'" From the novel *The Fast Buck,* James Hadley Chase, 1952
Top eliminator	The fastest hotrod, or hotrod driver, total shutdown artist
Top storey	Head, brain
Top stud	The leader, the head honcho, the boss
Too much	The best, really good, a total knockout See the vocal group recording *Much Too Much*, The Hollywood Flames, 1959
Torn up	Wasted, upset, ragged, unsettled, maybe impressed
Torpedo	Gunman, hitman
Torso-tosser	Hootchie-coochie dancer, strip artist
Tough enough to swap punches with a power shovel	Hard, resilient, not exactly a pushover
Tramp on it	Hurry up, get moving, go faster "Tramp on it, friend, make speed." From the novel *The Little Sister*, Raymond Chandler, 1949

191

Trash Gossip, chatter, loose talk

Trifling Unfaithful
"Who's been playin' around with you,
a real cool cat with eyes of blue?
Trifling baby are you being true,
who's been fooling around with you?"
From the rockabilly recording
Red Cadillac And Black Mustache,
Warren Smith, 1957

Trigger-man Assassin, hit-man
"He'd killed several men. Nobody knew
how many except George, and he probably couldn't count that high. He'd been a
trigger-man for a couple of the top men of
the U.S. crime syndicate, and was noted
for his efficiency and stupidity."
From the novel *Darling, It's Death,*
Richard S. Prather, 1953

Trottery Dancehall
Troubled with the Broke, poverty-stricken
shorts From the autobiography *Really The
Blues*, Mezz Mezzrow and Bernard Wolfe,
1946

Trucking 1. Fucking
See the blues recordings *Let's Get Drunk
And Truck,* The Harlem Hamfats, 1936;
Caught My Gal Truckin', Tampa Red,
1936; and the country recording *Can't
Nobody Truck Like Me*, Cliff Bruner's
Texas Wanderers, 1937

2. A dance made popular at the Cotton
Club in Harlem in the early 1930s
"'Aw, come on, Camelia,' called Miss
Day, moving her torso slowly from side to
side. 'I'd like to do a little truckin'.'"
From the novel *The Dead Don't Care,*
Jonathan Latimer, 1937

3. Walking

"Truck on down and dig me, Jack . . ."
From the R&B jump jive recording
Five Guys Named Moe, Louis Jordan &
The Tympany Five, 1942

Trust
"I trusted Amy about as far as I could
have pushed the tractor and trailer with
two broken legs."
From the novel *The Lady Is A Lush*,
Orrie Hitt, 1960

Tuckered out
Worn out, exhausted

Tucson blanket
A newspaper, the usual item of hobo
bedding, also known as a California blanket

Turn on the phonograph
Confess to the police

Turn the duke
Short change someone

Turning your damper down
Sexually satisfied
See the country recording
I Think I'll Turn Your Damper Down,
Jimmie Davis, 1937

"With a blonde-headed woman
you need to get around,
but a black haired girl
will turn your damper down."
From the rockabilly recording
Forty Nine Women,
Jerry Irby & The Texas Ranchers, 1956

Twicin'
1. Cheating on your partner, sleeping
with two people at once

2. Doublecrossing

Twist
Woman, dame, doll
"The twist might die . . . there was a
prowl car not more than ten yards away.
I had to hit her."
Yet another James Hadley Chase

193

character comes over all chivalrous and
sensitive.
From the novel *The Fast Buck*, 1952

Two-bit porch climber   Low-class house burglar

Two hands full of piano   A damn good player, hot stuff at whippin' that ivory
"He had the beat to steady down a little combination, just like a good drummer. He really kept two hands full of piano."
From the novel *Blues For The Prince*, Bart Spicer, 1950

Typewriter   Machine gun

Ufftay — Tough

Ultimate yelp — Superlative, the best
"She is the last word – the ultimate yelp."
From the novel *Your Deal My Lovely*,
Peter Cheyney, 1941

Under glass — In prison

Underpinning — Legs

Undertaker's friend — Gun, firearm

Unglued — Worked up, losing it, flipping your wig
Elvis kisses his co-star, then asks:
"How's your headache?", to which she
replies, "I'm coming all unglued..."
From the film *Jailhouse Rock*, 1957

Unhook your ears, Dad — Listen closely
From the film *Shake, Rattle And Rock*,
1957

Unwound — Losing it, falling to pieces, cracking up

Up jumped the devil — An unexpected piece of bad fortune
"Then up jumped the devil, like the crap-
shooters say when seven pops up
wrong."
From the autobiography *Rap Sheet*,
Blackie Audett, 1955

Up north — In jail
"Pimping will get you a couple of years
up north."
From the novel *The Drowning Pool*,
Ross MacDonald, 1950

Upping some real crazy riffs — Playing cool music

Uptight   1. Worried, tense

                              2. In trouble

Used-to-be   Ex-lover
                              See the blues recording
                              I'm Going Back To My 'Used to Be',
                              Bessie Smith & Clara Smith, 1924

                              "You say you're through with me,
                              You're settin' me free,
                              You're just out with your used-to-be,
                              I can't hardly stand it, you troublin' me,
                              I can't hardly stand it, it just can't be.
                              Well you don't know babe I love you so
                              You got me all tore up, all tore up . . ."
                              From the rockabilly recording
                              I Can't Hardly Stand It,
                              Charlie Feathers, 1956

V

Vag

Vagrant, hobo, bum
"Look at you, all bunged-up like a barrel-house vag ..."
The police captain takes a dim view of the battered appearance of one of his detectives.
From the film *Where The Sidewalk Ends*, 1950

Vamoose

Run away, leave in a hurry, get lost

Varicose alley

Stripclub runway

Vines

Suits, jackets, hipster threads
Babs Gonzales tells the story in his 1967 autobiography (*I, Paid My Dues*) of how Charlie Parker apologised for stealing some of his suits: "Babs, baby, I know I downed your threads, so here's the tickets."
ie: I stole your clothes, and here are the pawnshop tickets.

Viper

Marijuana smoker
See the jazz recordings *The Viper's Drag*, Cab Calloway & his Orchestra, 1930; *Song of the Vipers*, Louis Armstrong & his Orchestra, 1934; *Sendin' The Vipers*, Mezz Mezzrow Orchestra, 1934

Vomit on the table

Speak up, let's hear what you've got to say
"Come on, fess up. Vomit on the table ..."
From the novel *Go, Man, Go!*, Edward De Roo, 1959

Voodoo boilers

A kit of drums

W

Wail

Cut loose, let off steam, have a wild time
"Now, if you're gonna stay cool, you've got to wail, you've got to put something down, you've got to make some jive. Do you know what I'm saying?"
Marlon Brando tells it like it is.
From the film *The Wild One*, 1954

Waffle iron

The electric chair

Walking papers

Release from jail

Walking spanish

Being frogmarched out of somewhere

Wanna oil your ankles?

Would you care to dance?

Want a real rear?

Do you want something that'll really get you high?
"'Want a real rear?' she inquired. 'Laudanum?'
'Yeah. A dash with the next whisky.'"
From the novel *Red Gardenias*, Jonathan Latimer, 1939

Want a weed?

Would you like a cigarette?

Warble

Sing
"They do tell me lots of dames make the grade if they can warble a few notes and if they can show a shapely pair o' gams."
From the novel *Hot Dames On Cold Slabs*, Michael Storme, 1950

Phonograph Monthly Review from New York ran a Miscellaneous Warblers column in its dance music reviews section in the early 1930s.

Watch my smoke

I'm outta here, I'm gone

Ways like a mowing machine

Agricultural metaphor for good sexual technique

"She's long, she's tall,
She's a handsome queen,
She's got ways like a mowing machine."
From the country recording
She's A Hum Dum Dinger, Buddy
Jones, 1941
Compare this to the blues recording
I've Got Ford Movements In My Hips,
Cleo Gibson & her Hot Three, 1929

Wax a disc   To make a recording

Wear the green   Have some paper money

Wearing a concrete footmuff   Taking a swim in the river with your feet encased in concrete, courtesy of the Mafia

Wearing lead buttons on your vest   Getting shot
"'Talk like that to me,' Morny said
"and you are liable to be wearing lead buttons on your vest.'"
From the novel *The High Window*,
Raymond Chandler, 1943

Weedhead   Cannabis smoker
See the blues recording *Weedhead Woman*, Champion Jack Dupree, 1939

Week at the knees   Unsuccessful courtship
eg: "Man, I spent a week at the knees once, never got any further."

Weiner   Penis
In Nelson Algren's 1941 novel *Never Come Morning*, the prostitute Tooki asks a prospective client "Ain't you gonna play Hide The Weenie, Hon? C'mon, Slim, let's slam it around a little."

"Some said it takes hot water
Baby can't you see,
But your heat baby
Is plenty warm enough for me,
Baby please warm my weiner . . ."
From the blues recording

199

Please Warm My Weiner,
Bo Carter (Bo Chatman), 1936

Wet your tonsils   Drink

What do you shake them for?   How do you earn a living? What's your occupation?

What do you think of the stackup?   How does the situation appear to you?

What know, man?   Hipster form of greeting
From the autobiography *I, Paid My Dues*, Babs Gonzales, 1967

What's all the shooting about?   What's up? Why the fuss?
From the film *Don't Knock The Rock*, 1956

What's on the agenda, Brenda?   What's happening? How are you doing?

What's the belch, friend?   What's happening? What's the news?
From the novel *Halo In Blood*, Howard Browne, 1946

What's cookin'? Nothin' but spaghetti, and it ain't ready   Nothing's happening, I don't have any news

What's the good word?   What's happening? What's the news?
Used by Dashiell Hammett in the novel *The Glass Key*, 1931

What's the pitch?   What's the story? What's happening?

What's tickin', chicken?   What's happening? How are you?

Wheel a spiel   Make a speech, talk big

When they made you, they scraped off the mould   You're a louse, you're the lowest of the low

Where do you hang your hat?	Where are you from? Where are you staying?
Whippin' that ivory	Playing the piano
A whiskey sour to all the beer in Brooklyn	A dead cert, a sure thing
Whisper	Rumour, news
Whistle bait	A good-looking woman, someone worth whistling at "Her name was Rhoda Stern. She didn't have to tell us that she wasn't whistle bait, if she ever had been." From the novel *The Lenient Beast*, Fredric Brown, 1957
Whistling through the graveyard	Bluffing, putting up a front "Phil Duncan slid two blue chips into the centre of the table. 'Two blues say you're whistling through the graveyard.'" From the novel *This Is Murder*, Erle Stanley Gardner, 1935
Who broke your doll?	Why are you crying? "'What's the pitch, bitch?' I demanded. 'Who broke your doll?'" Matt Helm comes over all sensitive and concerned, from the novel *Murderer's Row*, Donald Hamilton, 1961
Wholesale banking business	Bank robbery
Whoopee	Mostly this was a euphemism for sex, although it was also taken more generally to mean having a good time, whooping it up "Most always when a man leaves his wife, there's no excuse in the world for him. She may have been making whoop-whoop-whoopee with the whole ten commandments, but if he shows his

disapproval to the extent of walking out on her, he will thereafter be a total stranger to all his friends."
From the short story *Ex Parte*, Ring Lardner, 1920s

"Lonnie Johnson goes in for the fantastically macabre in his blues *She's Making Whoopee In Hell Tonight* and *Death Valley Is Half Way To My Home*."
From the magazine *Phonograph Monthly Review*, New York, April 1930

"I was out last night
At the cabaret,
Came in this morning
'Bout the break of day
Been makin' whoopee ..."
From the blues recording *Tight Whoopee*, Mozelle Alderson, 1930

See the jazz song *Makin' Whoopee*, written by Walter Donaldson in 1928, for the Broadway show *Whoopee!*

Whoopee mama   Good-time girl, flapper, party animal

Why did you do me this way?   How could you treat me like that?

Wide-open town   Wild, lawless, packed with late-night entertainment
"Aw, come on, man. Have a couple of drinks and you'll feel better. This is a wide-open town."
From the novel *The Drowning Pool*, Ross MacDonald, 1950

Wig   1. Head or hair
See the jazz recording *Gassin' The Wig*, Roy Porter, 1948

2. Mind

Wig chop   A haircut

Wig out	Go crazy, have a wild time, enjoy
Wig tightener	Something, or someone, very impressive
Wiggle	Dance, strut your stuff "She's got a wiggle Make a dead man awake, She don't rock She just stands there and shakes." From the rockabilly recording *My Baby Don't Rock*, Luke McDaniel, 1957
Windy	Scared, apprehensive
Wine Spo-Dee-O-Dee	An obscene U.S. army drinking song The lyrics were cleaned up slightly by Stick McGhee for his 1949 R&B record- ing entitled *Drinking Wine Spo-Dee-O- Dee*. The original lyric went "Drinking wine, motherfucker, drinking wine . . ." By the time Jack Kerouac got around to including the term in his novel *On The Road* (1957), it had somehow become just another name for a drink: "Dean and I had ended up with a coloured guy called Walter who ordered drinks at the bar and had them lined up and said 'Wine-spodiodi!' which was a shot of port wine, a shot of whisky, and a shot of port wine. 'Nice sweet jacket for all that bad whisky!' he yelled."
Wino time	A short jail sentence
Wiper	Assassin, hitman, rub-out artist
Wise guy	1. Mobbed up, a made man, a member of the Mafia 2. Smart aleck "'A wise guy!' Bert commented, slapping me across the face . . ." From the novel *Two Timing Tart*, John Davidson, 1961

Wise up	1. Get smart
	2. To educate or inform someone
Woo number	Girlfriend or boyfriend
Wooden kimono	Coffin
Woodpile	Xylophone
Woodshed	"A place for a private rehearsal, often used as a verb, meaning to practise in private." From *Down Beat's Yearbook Of Swing*, 1939
Wordsville	A library "Look out, or we'll be thrown out of Wordsville." From the novel *Run Tough, Run Hard*, Carson Bingham, 1961
Working for the Woolworths	Doing a low-paid job, ie: for nickels & dimes
Working your groundsmashers overtime	1. Moving fast
	2. Dancing in an impressive fashion
Wouldst like to con a glimmer early with me this black?	Would you like to go to a movie with me this evening? From Professor Cab Calloway's Swingformation Bureau.
Wound up like an eight-day clock	Uptight, tense, stressed out
Wrecking crew	Police interrogation operatives "Take this baby down the cellar and let the wrecking crew work on him before you lock him up." From the novel *Red Harvest*, Dashiell Hammett, 1929 *The Wrecking Crew* was the title of a

novel from 1960 which was part of Donald Hamilton's Matt Helm series, the film versions of which starred Dean Martin, and it was also the collective name for the regular musicians who played on Phil Spector's Wall Of Sound recordings in the early Sixties.

A wrong gee   A bad sort, an untrustworthy guy

Wrong side of the tracks   The bad part of town, lowdown, poverty row

X-ray eyes

"Either we got x-ray eyes, or those babies are dancing in their underwear."
The lure of the taxi-dancehall becomes apparent to a first-time customer.
From the novel *The Lady In The Morgue*, Jonathan Latimer, 1936

Yak

Talk
"If there's anything I can't stand, it's a cheap jerk who yakkity-yaks all the time. Kick him in the teeth if he keeps talking, Pete."
From the novel *The Deadly Lover*, Robert O. Saber, 1951

"I was so stunned I let him keep on yakking."
From the novel *Always Leave 'Em Dying*, Richard S. Prather, 1961

Yammer

Talk

Yap

1. Talk

2. Mouth
eg: "Shut your yap."

Yard

One hundred dollars
After 1930 it often meant one thousand dollars.

Yas Yas Yas

Ass, backside
"I used to play slow but now I play it fast, just to see the women shake their yas, yas, yas . . ."
From the blues recording *Shack Bully Stomp*, Peetie Wheatstraw, 1938

See also the blues recordings
The Duck's Yas Yas Yas, James Stump Johnson & Alex Hill, 1929 and *Yas Yas Yas Number 1,* Jimmy Strange (The Yas Yas Man), 1936

Yaks

Laughs, fun
"We had a lotta yaks, huh Johnny?"
From the film *The Wild One*, 1954

Yegg	1. Criminal. Originally this was a specific term for a safe-cracker, but came to have a more general use "The big man was a yegg. San Fransico was on fire for him." ie: He was a criminal, and he was the object of a city-wide manhunt. From the short story *Fly Paper*, Dashiell Hammett, 1920s "The dame shrugged her bare shoulders. 'You know it all, mac. Sure, my old man was a gangster, a tough yegg . . .'" From the novel *The Corrupt Ones*, J.C. Barton, crica 1950 2. A beggar
You ain't just whistling Dixie	That's right, I agree with you, you're speaking the truth
You are a triple scream and one big yell	I really like you
You burn me up	1. You excite me 2. You make me angry See the jazz recording *Cold Mamas Burn Me Up*, Bailey's Lucky Seven, 1924
You can cook him up brown	You can get your own back, you can have your revenge "If you want to get back at him, here's your chance. You can cook him up brown." From the novel *Violent Night*, Whit Harrison, 1952
You can sing two choruses of that	You can say that again
You can take that to the bank and cash it	It's the truth, I mean it, this is reliable information

208

You fracture me	You make me laugh "'You fracture me, Elmer,' she said. 'To look at you, a person would think you just came in with a car-load of cattle.'" From the novel *Little Men, Big World,* W.R. Burnett, 1951
You give me hot pants	I find you very attractive
You got any happy money on you?	It'll cost you "'You got any happy money on you?' 'Happy money?' 'Yeah. Money that's gonna make me happy, what else?' 'How much?' 'Fifty dollars.'" From the film *Pickup On South Street,* 1953
You jet me	You're the most, I'm really impressed "You positively jet me! Gone, gone, gone! Jet, jet, jet!" From the novel *Go, Man Go!,* Edward De Roo, 1959
You paralyse me	You make me laugh, you surprise me, you knock me out
You said a mouthful	That's the truth, that's it exactly
You send me	I'm gone, you flip me out, I'm impressed See the ballad *You Send Me,* Sam Cooke, 1957 "Every time she loves me She sends my mellow soul." From the boogie-woogie recording *Roll 'Em, Pete,* Pete Johnson & Joe Turner, 1938
You send me to the end	You *really* send me

You snap the whip, I'll make the trip	I'll do what you say, I'm all yours
You'd better get your flaps down or you'll take off	Don't get so excited, calm down From the first film version of *Farewell, My Lovely*, 1944
You'll find my name on the tail of my shirt	Traditional response to police questioning, especially by tramps and drifters "Told them my name was on the tail of my shirt, I'm a Tennessee hustler, I don't have to work …" From the country recording *T for Texas (Blue Yodel No. 1)*, Jimmie Rodgers, 1927
Your brain's a little dusty	You're rather stupid, you're not thinking straight
Your roof is leaking	You're not all there, you're a little crazy
Your teeth are swimming	You're plastered, you're full up with booze "You're drunk, Al. Your teeth are swimming." From the novel *What Makes Sammy Run?*, Budd Schulberg, 1941
You're a panic	You crack me up, you're really funny
You're killing me with your sad pan	Why the long face, you look depressed
You're my habit, rabbit	I dig you the most
You're not comin' through at all	You're making no sense, explain yourself
You're not just saying it	That's right, I agree with you

You're stepping on your motor to hear your cut-out roar	You're bragging, you're all talk
You're talking on a dead phone	I'm not interested, save your breath
You're the swinging end	You're the best
You've got a crust	You've got a nerve "You've got a hell of a crust assuming I'll go down there and take a getaway stake to somebody I know the police are looking for." From the novel *The Lady in the Lake,* Raymond Chandler, 1944 "'To hell with you,' she blazed. 'You got a crust, tearing my clothes like that.'" From the novel *Homicide Lost*, William Vance, 1956
You've got a date with the fireless cooker	They're going to send you to the electric chair
You've got my nose wide open	You've got me all worked up "'You'd better take it easy from now.' 'That's what I intend to do, only trouble is m'nose opens up and I can't tell what I'm doing.'" From the novel *On The Road*, Jack Kerouac, 1957 See the R&B recording *When It Rains It Really Pours,* Billy The Kid Emerson, 1955 Also the vocal group recording *She's Got his Nose Wide Open,* Ike Perry & The Lyrics, 1960
You've had your chance and folded	You wasted the opportunity, you blew it

211

Z

Zip gun   Home made pistol, Saturday night special

Zip your lip   Keep quiet

Zoot suit   Draped and sculpted hepcat suit
Long in the body, narrow at the waist, as worn by his Royal Hepness,
Cab Calloway, onstage at Harlem's
Cotton Club. Very popular with the
Chicano gangs in Los Angeles during the early stages of World War Two, memorably described by James Ellroy in his novel *The Black Dahlia* as "Reet-pleat, drape-shape, stuff-cuff, Argentinian-duck-tailed Mexican gangsters." This type of clothing was condemned by Government officials as a waste of cloth and counter-productive to the war effort. A particularly brutal series of gang rumbles which broke out in 1943 were known in the press as the Zoot Suit Wars.

"The young hoodlums wore long coats, pegged pants and droooping keychains.
They were about eighteen.
They looked out at the world coldly and arrogantly. A tough place, chum! But we're tougher."
From the novel *Little Men, Big World*,
W.R. Burnett, 1951

See the jazz recording *A Zoot Suit (For My Sunday Gal)*,
Bob Crosby & his Orchestra, 1942